PORTFOLIO

THE DUMBEST MOMENTS IN BUSINESS HISTORY

Adam Horowitz is the deputy editor of *Business 2.0* and a creator of "The 101 Dumbest Moments in Business," one of the magazine's most popular annual features. He and his fellow editors are based in San Francisco. Which is good, because a number of restaurants in his former home of Santa Fe—in not-at-all-dumb moments of business judgment—have banned him for publicly ridiculing their shortcomings.

Visit *Business 2.0* online at www.business2.com.

The Dumbest Moments
in Business History

USELESS PRODUCTS,
RUINOUS DEALS,
CLUELESS BOSSES
AND OTHER SIGNS OF
UNINTELLIGENT LIFE IN THE
WORKPLACE

**Adam Horowitz
and the Editors of *Business 2.0*
Compiled by Mark Athitakis
and Mark Lasswell**

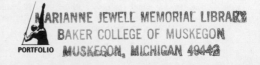

PORTFOLIO
Published by the Penguin Group
Penguin Group (USA) Inc., 375 Hudson Street, New York, New York 10014, U.S.A.
Penguin Group (Canada), 10 Alcorn Avenue,Toronto, Ontario, Canada M4V 3B2
(a division of Pearson Penguin Canada Inc.)
Penguin Books Ltd, 80 Strand, London WC2R 0RL, England
Penguin Ireland, 25 St Stephen's Green, Dublin 2, Ireland
(a division of Penguin Books Ltd)
Penguin Group (Australia), 250 Camberwell Road, Camberwell,
Victoria 3124, Australia (a division of Pearson Australia Group Pty Ltd)
Penguin Books India Pvt Ltd, 11 Community Centre,
Panchsheel Park, New Delhi – 110 017, India
Penguin Group (NZ), cnr Airborne and Rosedale Roads,
Albany, Auckland, New Zealand (a division of Pearson New Zealand Ltd)
Penguin Books (South Africa) (Pty) Ltd, 24 Sturdee Avenue,
Rosebank, Johannesburg 2196, South Africa

Penguin Books Ltd, Registered Offices:
80 Strand, London WC2R 0RL, England

First published in the United States of America by
Portfolio, a member of Penguin Group (USA) 2004
This paperback edition published 2005

1 3 5 7 9 10 8 6 4 2

Illustrations by Mark Matcho

Published in arrangement with Eye Candy Books LLC, 23 Bank Street,
New York, New York 10014,
under the stern direction of Jessica Marshall, Ph.D.

THE LIBRARY OF CONGRESS HAS CATALOGED THE HARDCOVER EDITION AS FOLLOWS:
Horowitz, Adam, 1968–
The dumbest moments in business history ; useless products, ruinous deals,
clueless bosses and other signs of unintelligent life in the workplace / by Adam
Horowitz and the editors of *Business 2.0*.
p. cm.
Includes index.
ISBN 1-59184-035-X (hc.)
ISBN 1-59184-067-8 (pbk.)
1. Industrial management—History—Anecdotes. 2. Business failures—History—
Anecdotes. 3. Business history—Anecdotes. I. Business 2.0 (2001). II. Title.
HD31.H6497 2004
338.09—dc22   2003063264

Printed in the United States of America
Set in Avenir
Designed by Erin Benach

Contents

Welcome to *The Dumbest Moments in Business History*. This volume is a collection of cautionary tales from which we all can learn valuable lessons about how *not* to conduct business. So I'm pretty certain you can expense it.

I'm not sure why people love to read about stupidity in business, but they do. I know this because every year, our magazine, *Business 2.0,* features the "101 Dumbest Moments in Business," and readers go crazy for it. Perhaps it's the same impulse that makes bloopers such a whoop-de-do in the sports roundup on the nightly news. Or maybe it's more like rubbernecking. I try not to think about either too much. All I know is, it works. When we ran "101 Dumbest Moments" last year, TV crews came from as far away as the Netherlands to interview our writers. I guess they don't actually do enough business over there to generate their own dumb moments.

On the pages that follow, you'll find examples of stupidity so monumental, they'll make your head spin like the hood ornament of an Edsel (before it flies into the windshield). I can't promise that this book will inoculate you from business idiocy. But if you like bloopers, you're in for one heck of a read.

ORGANIZATIONAL CONCEIT EXPLAINED

The following tales of jaw-dropping imbecility are arranged in chapters corresponding to the divisions of a corporate organization to make it easy and fun to follow the trajectory of dim-bulb behavior through the hallways of the workaday world—and because otherwise the book would be just a grab-bag of business idiocy, a riot of terrible products, self-destructive advertising, untalented fraud artists, spectacularly misjudged mergers, swinging-dick interoffice braggadocio, money-flushing Hollywood movies, squandered fortunes, flubbed opportunities and bogus sex aids. Which, come to think of it, is a pretty good snapshot of the witless underside of the world economy ever since the Industrial Revolution.

Nevertheless, like wine experts savoring the differences among grape-growing regions, we aficionados of dumb moments in business are able to classify and relish the distinctions between, say, boneheaded moves in accounting (seemingly dry and monochromatic, these screw-ups build in flavor over time, leaving a powerfully expensive aftertaste) and moronic manufacturing decisions (a woody presence with metallic undertones, accented with lots of fruity depositions).

Of course, some idiotic incidents resist categorization because truly dumb moments in business often are an ensemble effort. Why else would people spend so much time in meetings? In these cases, using the combination of expertise and utter whim that we employ throughout the book, we award the dunce cap to whichever department we feel like picking on.

CRITERIA FOR INCLUSION

First of all, nobody gets killed. When idiocy trips over into lethality—the exploding Ford Pinto comes to mind—only the truly twisted can get a giggle out of it. So consider yourself warned, sicko.

Second, the stories must have a discernible moment of utter fatuity rather than a slowly festering brainlessness. You try to make something funny out of the Bank of Credit and Commerce International.

Third, when some form of business buffoonery is particularly chronic, only the choicest example makes the cut. For instance, private-sector types who enter government and regard it as a colossal piggybank are all too familiar, so we picked our favorite: William Duer, the assistant secretary of the Treasury who looted a fortune from the tender young U.S. government after the Revolutionary War and managed to end up in debtor's prison nevertheless. With a guy like that, do you really need to hear about Spiro Agnew?

APOLOGIES TO THE SLIGHTED

No doubt the government of Bahrain will lodge a protest that they once had a crook who was much stupider and more colorful than Duer and therefore deserves the "dumbest" distinction. Yes, you will detect an emphasis toward homegrown American chowderheads and toward incidents from the United States in the past half-century. But it's not so much a case of provincialism as the simple fact that the most powerful economic engine the world has ever known inevitably produces an inordinate amount of industrial waste in the form of really dumb folks doing really dumb things.

That said, we welcome your scathing criticism and urgent additions. After all, we're already collecting entries for the *New! Updated! Dumbest Moments in Business History*. What do you think we are—*stupid*?

INTRODUCTION TO THE
PAPERBACK EDITION

It's been less than a year since the hardcover edition of this book was published, and we're happy to report that it worked. The world's business leaders and their rank-and-file drones pored over these cautionary tales of greed, sloth, and incompetence and came away with a crash-course education in how to avoid perpetrating the next Edsel, New Coke, or 23-pound Osborne "portable" computer. Thanks to our efforts, good ol' American-style capitalism will now sail into a future that's completely cleared of the shoals of stupidity that brought us, well, Kevin Costner's *Waterworld*.

Not buying it? Good, then you've purchased the right book. Making outrageous, unsupportable claims about our product would be terribly, terribly dumb—but hey, not as dumb as some of the other media gaffes committed in 2004. One that comes immediately to mind—okay, that comes from the folder where we at *Business 2.0* smirkily accumulate these anecdotes all year long in preparation for our wildly popular annual feature, "The 101 Dumbest Moments in Business"—is the recipe published by a large-circulation U.S. lifestyle magazine that, when followed to the letter, would ignite a rather impressive kitchen fire. Then there was the leading British hiking magazine that provided readers with published trail directions, which—again, if followed to the letter—would have sent them straight over the edge of a cliff.

Thankfully, the goofs by our brothers in the media have been no match for those of big business. Witness cell phone maker Nokia, which recently sent out a text message to its customers inviting them to a gathering at a major trade show. Unfortunately, the act of opening the message instantly disabled the phones of hundreds of Nokia users. Hormel Foods was forced to recall 104,000 pounds of Stagg Chili—"Hearty Beef with a Kick of Green Chilies," to be precise—after the kick turned out to come instead from the ground-up parts of a plastic handheld calculator. Taco Bell found itself getting kicked around, too, after one of its restaurant managers—responding to a prank phone call from a man claiming to be a police officer—strip searched a 17-year-old female customer. At least he didn't do it at gunpoint. That must have been a relief to handgun maker Smith & Wesson, which is dedicated to the *lawful* use of firearms. How do we know this? Because the company's own chairman resigned in 2004 after newspaper reporters discovered that, before becoming a corporate exec, he'd spent 15 years in prison for a string of armed robberies and an attempted prison escape.

So, yes, given the evidence above, we freely admit that this book apparently has been an utter flop at helping the business world avoid committing the corporate equivalent of torching its own kitchens and stepping off of cliffs. *What a relief.*

The Dumbest Moments in Business History

RESEARCH AND DEVELOPMENT

[A bad idea has to start somewhere. It's that old business maxim: You can't make a defective omelet without designing a really inefficient, expensive and dangerous way of breaking some eggs. Welcome to R&D.]

Thanks, but We're Happy with the Double Entendres We Get in Beer Commercials.

"If a cheerleader, for argument's sake, introduces a tight end . . . there may be a little double entendre. Not unsavory, but things that are different from the NFL."

—World Wrestling Federation chairman Vince McMahon, explaining how research and development for the XFL, a supposed rival for the NFL created in collaboration with NBC, came up with a few new wrinkles for pro football. The league folded in 2001 after one season and a $100 million investment, but left its mark on television: one game broadcast was believed to be the lowest-rated prime-time program ever.

Hellbent for Pleather

The 1964–65 World's Fair was a veritable cavalcade of ingenuity. IBM was showing off the latest in mainframe computer technology. RCA was broadcasting TV shows—in color! NASA brought in a full-size, first-stage Saturn V rocket. Impressive stuff.

Oh, and DuPont had a musical about Corfam.

The Wonderful World of Chemistry was actually about all sorts of DuPont products. As smiley actors and actresses sang "The Happy Plastic Family," audience members sat in Antron-Fabrilite chairs on Nylon carpets, watching the performers in front of a Mylar curtain. But Corfam, a new synthetic leather, was the star of the show. Promoted as having the feel and durability of leather, Corfam shoes also were water-repellent and were supposed to never need shining—attributes that inspired DuPont to proclaim that soon 25 percent of America's footwear would be made of Corfam. But then the other shoe dropped: The plastic was so unyielding that you could never, ever, break in a pair of Corfam shoes. People hated 'em. After seven years, DuPont told its wonder shoe to take a walk, at a cost of $100 million.

Try Our New Cigarette: All the Foul Taste You Expect, Plus the Aroma of Squandered Millions.

"A new era for smoking is about to begin," announced RJ Reynolds Tobacco in an ad for its Premier cigarette in 1988. Yes, and the new era lasted, oh, about 16 weeks.

Developed under the code name Project Spa (sounds refreshing, no?), the Premier was RJ Reynolds' attempt to create a "smokeless" cigarette, designed to shut up the worrywarts who were starting to make a nuisance of themselves with warnings about the dangers of secondhand smoke. Though the Premier would feature all of the lung-corroding toxins that generations of smokers had come to love, it was promoted as a "cleaner" cigarette. Development and promotional costs reached $68 million, enraging the company's board of directors, who hadn't been informed of the Premier's existence until spending already had run amok.

There was scant evidence the product warranted the outlay. Even the company's own research reports didn't offer much support. The Premier might have looked out for the sensitivi-

3

ties of nonsmokers in the room, but it was hell on anyone who fired one up. Only 5 percent of smokers in an American focus group liked it. The smokeless cig even challenged the politeness of a Japanese test group, where one participant took a puff and reported, "This tastes like shit."

There was another problem, referred to by RJ Reynolds execs (they might make coffin nails, but who says they don't have a sense of humor?) as the "hernia effect." The Premier's smokeless design was so user-unfriendly that you practically needed a Dirt Devil to suck out the yummy nicotine-and-tar ambrosia. Smokers, never known for their prodigious lung power anyway, decided the Premier was itself a huge drag. Four months after the Premier's premiere, with tens of millions of dollars up in flames, RJ Reynolds discontinued the product, making the world safe again for unsafe cigarettes.

At Last, Nike Gives *Something* Back to the Third World.
Great innovations often result from asking the question "What if?" The invention of the Kenyan ski team started that way, too.

Looking for that last cranny of the world that hadn't been swooshed by the late 1990s, Nike hit on a novel brand-extension opportunity for the 1998 Winter Olympics in Nagano, Japan: what if the athletic shoe and clothing manufacturer secretly funded a training program to turn some of Kenya's fabled long-distance runners into cross-country skiers? Sort of a kicky new twist on the whole Jamaican-bobsled-team thing.

Spending about $250,000, Nike introduced two Kenyan runners, Henry Bitok and Philip Boit, to the pleasures of XC-skiing. The duo showed up in Nagano representing their country and keeping Nike's backing quiet. Bitok failed to qualify, but Boit managed to stumble to a last-place finish, 20 minutes behind the gold-medalist. Still, it made for a cute feel-good story about perseverance—at least until word of Nike's patronage leaked. Sports journalists turned the episode into a biathlon, pulling out their rifles to mix a little target practice with the skiing. One writer called Bitok and Boit "marketing pawns financed by well-heeled publicity seekers." Another dubbed Nike's machinations "Orwell at the Olympics."

"I can assure you that it is not a gimmick," said the chairman of the Kenyan National Olympic Committee. "You're going to hear a lot about Kenya and skiing." True enough. The water skiing near Mombasa is supposed to be terrific.

Great. That Means We'll Have to Pay Double for Light Switches, Too.

"They're multipurpose—not only do they put the clips on, but they take them off."

—Pratt & Whitney spokesperson Robert G. H. Carroll III, in 1990, explaining why it charged the Air Force $999.20 for a pair of pliers

No, That's Love in the Air. It Only *Smells* Like Butane.

The trouble with cigarette lighters is that they just don't lend themselves to lavish, Humvee-ish consumption of petroleum products. Oh, there was a spike back in the 1970s whenever Bob Dylan would keep 'em begging for encores till their BICs melted. But otherwise, it's just flick-flick and back in the pocket.

Don't blame Ronson. The folks at the butane and cigarette

lighter manufacturer took their shot at ramping up butane usage back in the 1960s, after looking over the sales numbers and deciding the fuel had so much more *potential.*

The boys in R&D came back with a device guaranteed to burn off a hell of a lot more lighter fluid than a chain-smoker could use in a week: the Ronson Veraflame. Priced at $30 and made from brushed aluminum, the Veraflame was a candle for hipsters who'd had it with antiquated wax technology. *This* flame, the ads bragged, was adjustable: "Low for intimate dinners. Medium for dinner parties . . . high for swinging soirees."

But then, as now, Americans were generally satisfied with the performance of the candles they had always used when they weren't just relying on electricity. And when they did just have the lights on, most folks were familiar with the dimmer-switch concept. And so the Veraflame slowly, sensually, odoriferously guttered out.

Katie, Your Party's Only Going to Last Two and a Half Minutes This Year If We're Going to Tape It. So Choose One: Clown or Cake?

By all accounts, Edwin Land was a genius 99 percent of the time. Land revolutionized photography—and minted money in the process—with the invention of instant color photographs in the 1960s. As the head of Polaroid in the 1970s, he acquired a reputation for being allergic to market research. He often guessed right, but unfortunately one of his most cherished ideas popped up while the nongenius one-percent window was open.

Land seemed to have convinced himself that the only way

he could top the invention of instant photos was to come up with the instant color movie. Proclaiming himself director of research on top of his CEO duties, Land approved $250 million in R&D funding to create his "living image system." He even plowed $68 million of his own cash into the project.

The result was the Polavision, introduced in 1978. The $700 contraption created instant movies, yes—but they only lasted two and a half minutes, ran without sound and required a special viewing device if you actually wanted to watch them. Which precious few people did. Sales were so slow during the Christmas season that Polaroid offered to have a Santa Claus hand-deliver a Polavision to anybody who bought one. Only 3,000 people signed up. And half of those clueless early-adapters probably thought they were buying into a bird's-eye view of Santa's workshop called Polarvision.

. . . Including the Pompous, Short-Sighted Bureaucrat

"Everything that can be invented has been invented."
—Federal Office of Patents commissioner Charles H. Duell, in 1899, declaring his job obsolete

But at Least They Canned the Ad with the Elephant and the Zookeeper.

Here's a fact we'll bet you're glad you didn't know: 63 percent of Americans use moist wipes or wet toilet paper while . . . well, let's put it this way, not while washing the car. Armed with this information, Kimberly-Clark thought it was sitting on a gold mine, sitting in the catbird seat, sitting pretty—well, we're almost certain that sitting or something that rhymes with it was involved. The company saw an enormous potential market of customers who at that point were improvising because nobody made the product they clearly yearned for. Dry toilet paper on a roll might have ruled the 20th century following its invention in 1890, but premoistened rolls would wipe up in the new century. The company poured $100 million into R&D, booked $35 million in advertising and in early 2001 proudly unfurled Cottonelle Fresh Rollwipes.

Maybe Kimberly-Clark thought the advantages of Rollwipes were self-evident and a grateful populace—nearly two-thirds of the country!—would reach for them instinctively. Otherwise, getting the word out was going to be tricky. One ad simply showed people happily splashing in a pool with the tagline "Sometimes wetter is better." Given that sort of vagueness, Cottonelle Fresh Rollwipes could've been a new kind of toilet paper or the worst-named water park in history.

With sales sluggish, a later print ad tiptoed toward frankness. It featured a sumo wrestler, shown from behind, with the wetter-better tagline. In an act of desperation, the company sent a van on the road with a restroom attached so that folks could privately test-drive Rollwipes. That's when Kimberly-Clark learned that people won't use PortaPotties unless somebody's sticking a gastrointestinal gun in their backs.

Clearly, toilet paper of any variety just isn't meant for blockbuster rollouts. After two years, Rollwipes was still languishing in test marketing and had a negligible impact on the company's (ahem) bottom line.

The Day Steve Jobs Went for a Stroll in the PARC and Ate Xerox's Lunch

Its official name was the Xerox Palo Alto Research Center, but it was more familiarly known simply as PARC. Nestled near the Stanford University campus and home to some of the most brilliant minds in technology research, Xerox PARC was the place where great ideas were invented—and then blithely given away.

Created in 1971, Xerox PARC was the copier company's attempt to work on technology transfer—birthing new innovations and bringing them to market. And by 1973 it had come up with some fascinating stuff. There was the Graphical User Interface (GUI), the computer mouse and the Ethernet to connect computers. But by 1979, Xerox still wasn't doing anything with these extremely cool ideas. That same year, a 24-year-old Steve Jobs, fresh from the success of his Apple 2 computer, visited the PARC complex.

Jobs, gawking at the GUI, begged his hosts to let him bring some Apple staffers back to check it out. A PARC administrator warned Xerox higher-ups that showing off the GUI would risk a tremendous asset, but his bosses said, in effect, "Oh, let Jobs ogle your little point-and-click OS toy all he wants . . . we're busy making copiers here." In the course of an hour-long demonstration to the Apple crew, Xerox successfully transferred their technology into the fertile minds of Jobs and his team. As Jobs later said, Xerox "could have owned the entire computer industry." Or was that what Bill Gates said about Steve Jobs?

Our Sexy New Shampoo, "Corporate Spy"—Now with the Scent of Half-Eaten Tuna Sandwiches!

Competing for market share can be a messy business, but some Procter & Gamble employees didn't get the memo explaining that they shouldn't take this idea too literally. In April 2001, P&G CEO John Pepper discovered that some staffers in his marketing department were too eagerly investigating the hair-care products of rival Unilever, going so far as to rifle through the garbage outside the company's Chicago offices. The Dumpster diving—or, as the corporate espionage folks call it, "waste archeology"—was part of a $3 million spying program that P&G initiated in the fall of 2000.

As R&D goes, the research was an unfortunate development. Though Pepper informed Unilever about his underlings' activities, P&G still had to pay out a reported $10 million to settle the matter. Three overzealous employees were fired, giving the garbage pickers the chance to spend some quality time in the tub testing the difference between P&G's Oil of Olay Moisturizing Body Wash and Nature's Breeze Body Wash, brought to you by Unilever.

Mr. Keely's Dynamic Turnkey Technology Solution

It's tempting to believe that the contemporary plague of mind-numbing corporate jargon is a novel form of mental illness that will fade away when people admit that burbling words such as *disintermediation* and *instantiation* just sounds silly. But, if history is any guide, polysyllabic claptrap will be with us as long as suckers are still regularly emerging from the delivery room.

Witness one John E. W. Keely, who in 1872 began exhibiting on the second floor of his Philadelphia home a curious device he'd developed. Having recently discovered a way to tap into the "inter-molecular vibrations of ether," Keely told onlookers, he had invented a "hydro-pneumatic-pulsating vacue" device that converted a quart of water into a fuel that offered a nearly endless supply of energy. In other, shorter words, Keely was saying he'd developed a perpetual-motion machine.

Investors, not looking into the part of Keely's résumé that read "carnival barker," were eager to invest. With the help of four businessmen—and $1 million—Keely organized the Keely Motor Company. His pitch to investors was as clear as an Enron bankruptcy filing: "With these three agents alone—air, water, and machine—unaided by any and every compound, heat, electricity, or galvanic action, I have produced in an unappreciable time by simple manipulation of the machine, a vaporic substance and one explusion . . ." and so on. Keely Motors never actually produced a Keely Motor, but its founder was able to put off questioners for years with his impenetrable wordsmithing. But finally, in 1899, a group of angry investors and reporters barged into Keely's house, where they discovered an array of hidden tubes, pipes and air compressors that created the illusion of perpetual motion. Before his accusers could apply their pneumatic-pulsating knuckles to his chin, though, Keely came down with pneumonia and lapsed into a state of perpetual inaction.

Sheesh, What're You Doing in There? Downloading *War and Peace*?

In the ongoing search to find ways to offer Internet access everywhere, all the time, Microsoft proudly announced that it had crossed connectivity's final frontier in the spring of 2003. The finest minds at the company's British branch had created the first Internet outhouse, iLoo, by "converting a portable loo to create a unique experience." Equipped with a Wi-Fi broadband connection, iLoo featured a flat plasma screen, a waterproof keyboard and toilet paper printed with Web site addresses. Six-channel surround-sound speakers were installed, ready to play your favorite, er, streaming audio tracks ("Splish Splash," say, or "I'm Coming Out").

The portable toilet was slated to make the rounds of British music festivals, but the gales of laughter that greeted the news prompted Microsoft's Redmond, Washington, headquarters to claim that the iLoo concept "was an April Fools joke"—which would have held more water if the company hadn't waited more than a month to let the world in on the supposed prank, and if the iLoo press release hadn't come out on April 30. With its credibility swirling around the bowl, Microsoft fessed up: iLoo was real, but still in the prototype stage. Acknowledging that iLoo "wasn't the best extension of our brand," Microsoft flushed the project.

And to Think, He Hadn't Even Heard of the iLoo Yet

"I can make a market on the Toilet Show. Contractors, interior designers and consumers could all tune in, and you know that you're talking to a group of people interested in toilets. With the efficiencies of distribution made possible by the Internet, you could make a business on that."

—Josh Harris, chairman of Web broadcast site Pseudo.com, speaking to *Adweek* in March 1999

Watch That Blood on the Footlights!

Transferring Stephen King's fiendishly well crafted horror tales to another medium is tricky. Sure, *Carrie* in 1976 and *Misery* in '90 were excellent skin-crawling movie theater experiences. But *The Langoliers* on TV in '95 was an unintentionally hideous experience.

For sheer adaptation lunacy, though, nothing could top *Carrie: The Musical* on Broadway in 1988. Out-of-town try-outs—the R&D of the theater business—couldn't have predicted the dubious honor that awaited this production.

"You can't deny that any show that begins with menstruation in the high school shower and ends with a double murder is obviously taking a risk," confessed artistic director Terry Hands. Right-o, Terry, we wouldn't think of denying it. The Royal Shakespeare Company production of the story of the awkward teen with telekinetic powers underwent multiple rewrites and delays, finally opening at the Virginia Theatre in May. The show was mercifully shuttered after just five performances.

Frank Rich, the *New York Times* theater critic at the time, advised readers that "those who have the time and money to waste on only one Anglo-American musical wreck on Broadway this year might well choose *Carrie*." Then Rich, aka "the Butcher of Broadway," tucked into the show's "uninhibited tastelessness," "whopping cliches," and "sub–Atlantic City costumes." That last one really had to sting. Having blown $8 million, the producers couldn't even top the outfits in a casino revue. But at least the outlay did buy them something: the record for most expensive flop in Broadway history.

But on the Plus Side, He Invented Vaudeville.

In 1760, Belgian inventor Joseph Merlin came up with the idea of attaching steel wheels to his boots, essentially inventing roller skates. Understandably proud of this accomplishment, he decided to introduce his million-dollar idea in grand style at a tony masquerade ball in London, but his decision to skate onto the dance floor while simultaneously playing a violin proved disastrous. Having overlooked the necessity to invent a braking device didn't help matters. An observer wrote that Merlin "impelled himself against a mirror, of more than five hundred pounds' value, dashed it to atoms, broke his instrument to pieces, and wounded himself most severely."

The Album So Nice AOL Time Warner Bought It Twice

One of the problems with managing a large corporation with dozens of subsidiaries is that it can be hard to keep track of exactly what the heck everybody's developing. And in 2001, AOL

Time Warner would have had to drill down pretty far to find that it was bringing along a Chicago rock band called Wilco. Tucked away with Reprise Records (a subsidiary of the Warner Music Group, itself a subsidiary of the company's Warner Bros. division), Wilco was beloved by critics, less so by music buyers. The band's previous album sold less than a half million copies. So when Wilco submitted its experimental *Yankee Hotel Foxtrot* album in the summer of 2001, the bosses at Reprise weren't hearing the platinum-promising CD they expected. Reprise demanded changes in the album; when Wilco refused, the label cut the band loose.

Wilco spent a few months in industry limbo, releasing *Foxtrot* songs as MP3 files on their Web site and being courted by new labels. In December 2001, the band finally settled on a contract with Nonesuch Records—which happened to be a subsidiary of a certain gigantic media company famous for its postmerger stock collapse. "If it doesn't bother AOL Time Warner, it doesn't bother me," said Wilco's frontman, Jeff Tweedy. "There's no way around the fact that they did in effect pay for the record twice."

Warner Music's press release did its best to find some positive spin, saying, "One of the advantages of having a company as large and diverse as W.M.G. is that when you have a fantastic band like Wilco, and one situation doesn't work out for one reason or another, they can continue to make this company their home."

Released in April 2002, *Yankee Hotel Foxtrot* earned rave reviews—and sold less than a half million copies.

Well, Tomorrow *Is* Another Day: Three Bad Calls on *Gone With the Wind.*

1. "Forget it, Louis. No Civil War picture ever made a nickel."
—MGM production executive Irving Thalberg in 1936, advising studio chief Louis B. Mayer not to bother buying the film rights to Margaret Mitchell's book

2. "I'm just glad it'll be Clark Gable who's falling flat on his face and not Gary Cooper."
—Gary Cooper, passing up the chance to play Rhett Butler

3. "This picture is going to be the biggest white elephant of all time."
—Director Victor Fleming, feeling savvy about demanding a flat fee for his work instead of taking the 20 percent of profits he'd been offered; *Gone With the Wind*'s worldwide box office earnings: more than $390 million

High Blood Pressure Problems? Try Liquid Paper!

In the 1980s, drug makers scrambled to develop a generic version of SmithKline Beecham's popular antihypertension drug Dyazide, but nobody could pull it off. A generic alternative would mean millions to the first one to crack the code. Then, in 1987, the Bolar company announced a breakthrough, won FDA approval and started milking its generic cash cow. Profits doubled to $31 million the following year. It was good news—followed by the bad news that a federal investigation had turned up a few odd touches in Bolar's FDA application. Test results indicating the drug's success were speckled with correction fluid, which concealed some actual, not-so-inspiring statistics. Oh, there were a few pages of undoctored, genuinely impressive test results that showed Bolar's product was just as effective as SmithKline Beecham's. But that's what you'd expect, since the numbers were lifted directly from SmithKline Beecham's paperwork.

After a failed attempt at stalling the feds, Bolar execs spent three years coping with indictments, depositions and other causes of high blood pressure. In 1991, Bolar admitted to fraud and price fixing, paying $10 million in fines and $20 million to angry shareholders. Within two years, fraud and corruption convictions had brought down eight Bolar managers, including CEO Robert Shulman, who was sentenced to five years and fined $1.25 million.

Realizing that its name would forever be associated with chicanery and the creative use of office supplies, Bolar changed its name to Circa. A dubious choice, given that "approximately" doesn't connote the sort of precision one likes to see in a pharmaceutical company, particularly one with a history of fudging results. But the company got off easy this time: in 1995, Circa became a wholly owned subsidiary of Watson Pharmaceuticals in a $595 million merger that practically whited-out the entire Bolar unpleasantness.

And What Would You Do with It Anyway, Feed It to the Horses? Haw-Haw-Haw.

"Oh, Townsend, oil coming out of the ground, pumping oil out of the earth as you pump water? Nonsense. You're crazy."

—The reported response when James Townsend sought the backing of New Haven bankers to drill for oil in the 1850s. On August 27, 1859, in Titusville, Pennsylvania, a Townsend well—and investors in his Seneca Oil Co.—hit a gusher.

They Were Sort of Like Mary Kay's Pink Cadillacs—Except Without the Air of Prosperity and Business Acumen.

Henry Ford may or may not have said that customers could buy his Model T in any color they wanted so long as it was black, but the line reflected the take-it-or-leave-it approach of the early days in automaking. By the 1950s, carmakers were tailoring product every way they could think of. In Chrysler's case, designers thought they saw a way to capitalize on the postwar surge in young married couples who were buying houses. Hmm . . . husbands and wives . . . two-car garages . . . how about his-'n'-her automobiles?

Chrysler unveiled the Le Comte and La Comtesse sedans at auto shows in 1954, with the she-car featuring a "gorgeous two-tone exterior of Dusty Rose with a Pigeon Grey top." Later retooled as the La Femme, the 1955 model featured a pink steering wheel and two-tone pink body, and was accessorized with a pink leather purse that included lipstick, a vanity mirror and a cigarette case. Pink raincoat and pink rain boots? Standard.

A year later, with La Femme sales alarmingly Le Thargic, Chrysler decided that its experts had misjudged what would appeal to those flighty female shoppers. Pink was so *wrong!* Enter, the 1956 La Femme, this time in lavender. "Designed exclusively for Her Royal Highness—the American Woman—this majestic beauty is rapidly approaching public announcement," read the marketing copy. Actually, the majestic beauty was about to be dethroned. After two years and about 1,000 sales, Chrysler admitted it had royally screwed up.

CHAPTER TWO

HUMAN RESOURCES

[Employees: A company's most valuable asset! Oh, that's just executive-suite propaganda. Try disposable pawns or ticking stupid bombs on for size.]

The Dumb Part Was Forgetting the 10 Percent Who Have 90 Percent of the Really, Really Sensitive Feelings.

"I don't want to sound heartless, but in almost every one of our businesses, there are 15 percent to 20 percent of the people that really add 80 percent of the value. Although we have a lot of good people, you can cut a fair amount and still be well positioned for the upturn."

—Goldman Sachs Group CEO Henry Paulson, discussing the investment banking firm's spate of layoffs at a January 2003 conference. A week later, Paulson sent a voicemail to Goldman employees apologizing for his remark.

Old Image Stirred by the Phrase *Job Action:* Samuel Gompers
New Image: Pee-wee Herman

Union members at the ARO car factory in Campulung, Romania, came up with a droll way of embarrassing the bureaucrats in Bucharest for failing to recruit investors after the business was privatized. In the fall of 2002, the workers announced that, in their desperation to save their jobs, they were going to raise money for the deep-in-debt factory by selling their sperm at $50 a pop to a local fertility clinic. A thousand men polishing more than chrome bumpers for a few months could raise some serious money. The stunt didn't prompt a sudden face-saving government subsidy, but it did win the ARO boys a worldwide reputation as a bunch of horny Romanians whose idea of united workers involves a bunch of guys sitting around the cafeteria and dreaming of Eva Herzigova.

Remember: If It Sounds Like Something Bluto Would've Done to Flounder, It's Probably Not an Enlightened Management Technique.

There are plenty of ways for companies to give employees incentives to step up productivity. Cash bonuses are nice. Stock options. Maybe a free vacation for a truly outstanding performance inspires the troops and gives 'em something to aim for.

At W.T. Grant department stores in the 1970s, the incentive was simple: hit your quotas and we won't humiliate you.

The department-store pioneer of the 1920s and the largest retailer in the country by the late '60s, W.T. Grant went hunting for new revenue streams in the '70s and discovered the magic of credit. Launching a massive push to sign up customers for W.T. Grant credit cards, the company knew that its managers were key to the project's success. So executives decided to ensure that the managers were out there flogging the card to customers. If they didn't bring in enough new applications, the managers were subjected to punishments that included being forced to use their noses to push peanuts across a floor, getting slapped in the face with pies and being forced to wear diapers.

The tactic worked so well that you could almost hear them debating in the W.T. Grant executive suite over whether investing in leather chaps and handcuffs would take productivity to the next level. It seemed like everybody in the world was buying crappy '70s clothes and gear with W.T. Grant cards. Credit purchases leaped to a quarter of the company's sales. But then, in 1974, the department-store chain learned what charities have known forever: that a pledge to pay is a lot different than actually forking over the dough. The company was forced to write off $94 million in losses from customers who wouldn't pay their charges. A year later the company declared bankruptcy. By early 1976, W.T. Grant and its 980 stores were no more. Which allowed a lot of embarrassed managers to wipe the pie off their faces while their bosses dealt with the egg on theirs.

He's a Seoulman and He Is KING, You Got That? Now Please Forward This Message.

E-mail. A boon to employees. So speedy. So efficient. So capable of causing embarrassment on a global scale. There's a reason why HR makes certain you get a little note explaining the proper uses of corporate e-mail when you show up for your first day on the job.

In the spring of 2001, Peter Chung was climbing the corporate ladder with impressive speed. A 24-year-old Princeton grad who started his career with Merrill Lynch, Chung was stationed in Seoul, South Korea, working for the Carlyle Group, a Washington, D.C., investment firm whose somber conservatism makes John Ashcroft look like Richard Simmons. He soon e-mailed a dozen friends about his new lifestyle:

So I've been in Korea for about a week and a half now and what can I say, LIFE IS GOOD. I've got a spanking brand new 2000 sq. foot 3 bedroom apartment with a 200-sq ft terrace running the entire length of my apartment with a view overlooking Korea's main river and nightlife.

Why do I need 3 bedrooms? Good question . . .

the main bedroom is for my queen size bed . . . where CHUNG is going to [expletive] every hot chick in Korea over the next 2 years (5 down, 1,000,000,000 left to go). . . the second bedroom is for my harem of chickies, and the third bedroom is for all of you [expletive] when you come out to visit my ass in Korea.

I go out to Korea's finest clubs, bars and lounges pretty much every other night on the weekdays and every day on the weekends too (I think in about 2 months, after I learn a little bit of the buy-side business I'll probably go out every night on the weekdays). I know I was a stud in NYC but I pretty much get about, on average, 5-8 phone numbers a night and at least 3 hot chicks that say that they want to go home with me every night I go out.

I love the buyside. I have bankers calling me every day with opportunities and they pretty much cater to my every whim—you know, golfing events, lavish dinners, a night out clubbing. The guys I work with are also all chill—I live in the same apartment building as my VP and he drives me around in his Porsche to work and when we go out. CHUNG is KING of his domain here in Seoul.

Oh, by the way, someone's gotta start FedExing me boxes of [condoms], I brought out about forty but I think I'll run out of them by Saturday.

Laters, Chung.

Aside from the problem of an innumerate investment expert (total population of South Korea: 47 million; number of [EXPLETIVE]-able hot chicks there? A bit short of "1,000,000,000"), Chung's braggadocio was so egregious that even his supposed pals couldn't believe it and started forwarding the e-mail with "Amazing Cautionary Tale" in the subject field. Chung was soon famous in financial circles around the world. His bosses at the Carlyle Group, unamused, neutered the stud's employment status, forcing him to resign two days later.

Mommy, Why Is Goofy Scratching Himself There?

June 6, 2001, dawned as another joyous day at Walt Disney World. Kids could squeal with glee on the roller coasters. Adults could have whimsical fun in the spinning teacups. And Mickey, Minnie, Donald and Pluto could wander the grounds, spreading goodwill without feeling the urge to paw their cartoonish crotches.

The preceding two months had seen tense negotiations between Disney and the Teamsters who play characters on the park's grounds, bargaining that had bared some unseemly details. The "cast members" weren't allowed to wear their own undergarments. Instead, they had to step into company-issued skivvies each day and leave them nightly with park employees for washing. Worse, the characters didn't have assigned undies. On any given day, Donald Duck might have to wear something used by Jiminy Cricket the day before. Teamsters reps claimed that Disney wasn't doing a thorough cleaning job and cited resulting cases of pubic lice and scabies.

Disney caved: each cast member would get his or her own set of undergarments and would be allowed to launder them at home—ending speculation that the Seven Dwarfs would be renamed Rashy, Blistery, Hivey, Licey, Twitchy, Buggy and Eczemie.

Timmy Can Have His Juice Box When Timmy Starts Hitting His Productivity Targets.

Chris Whittle, the CEO of Edison Schools Inc., realized in 2002 that his beleaguered education-for-profit enterprise was sitting on a personnel gold mine. Or, rather, the untapped workforce bonanza was sitting at school desks in Edison-operated outposts. The company's stock price had nose-dived from more than $20 to less than 50 cents as more and more school districts became less and less enthusiastic about privatized education, and Edison had been forced to sell off textbooks and lab materials to pay creditors.

Whittle floated his idea at a conference of educators. If students at Edison-run schools worked an hour per day in school offices for free, Whittle pointed out, it would take just 600 students to do the work of 75 adults. Think of the savings! Not that the kids wouldn't be reimbursed for their labors. They'd be paid handsomely with a valuable learning experience. Beats sitting around reading about Tom Sawyer's fence-painting operation.

"I think it's an important concept for education and economics," Whittle said.

The educators, perhaps familiar with all the bad press the coal-mining industry used to get for its child-labor practices, gave Whittle's proposition a big fat F.

As Opposed to the Something-Enormous Differential Between Red Sox and Yankees World Championships

"The price was something enormous, but I do not care to name the figures. No other club could afford to give the amount the Yankees have paid for him, and I do not mind saying I think they are taking a gamble."

—Boston Red Sox owner Harry Frazee in January 1920, explaining baseball's most infamous personnel move: selling Babe Ruth's contract to the New York Yankees for $100,000

Mariah, for the Thousandth Time, Where Is Your Company ID?

Folks who work in the human resources departments of music companies must say a small prayer every morning at the coffee machine, thanking God that pop stars don't count as actual employees. Otherwise, they'd have people like Mariah Carey flouncing into their cubicles every day and emotionally telling them, "Sometimes you just need a little therapy," instead of, as Carey did in July 2001, saving it for Carson Daly on MTV's *Total Request Live.*

Still, Carey's *Total* meltdown had to send a shudder through the offices of Virgin Records owner EMI Recorded Music. The singer—she of the glass-shattering high-end pipes and low-cut outfits—had just that spring signed one of the biggest recording contracts ever: $80 million, with $21 million up front, to record five albums for Virgin. Now she was burbling so incoherently on MTV that even the reliably unctuous Daly took a shot. "Ladies and gentlemen," he said, "Mariah Carey has lost her mind."

A few days later, Carey checked into rehab to deal with what her publicist called "an emotional and physical breakdown." But not before she had finished her first album under the contract, the soundtrack for the movie *Glitter,* which would feature Carey in her first starring role. The movie had the misfortune to be released a week after September 11, 2001, but it wasn't as if an instant classic would be overlooked during a time of national mourning. ("A vehicle that tarnishes as you watch it!"—*Chicago Tribune.* "An unintentionally hilarious compendium of time-tested cinematic clichés!"—*The New York Times.*) The soundtrack for the beleaguered movie sold a half million copies in the United States, a steep drop from Carey's usual multiplatinum heights.

In January 2002, EMI cut its losses, taking the extraordinary step of paying Carey $28 million to walk away. If the company looked dumb in 2001 for the over-the-top Carey contract, the possibility looms that the dumber move was dumping her. In December 2002, Carey released *Charmbracelet* for Island

Records. Sales in the first week of release were the second-best of her career, and by mid-2003, the album had more than doubled *Glitter*'s numbers, selling 1.1 million copies. And someone, somewhere, was relieved that he or she didn't have to figure out the FICA numbers on that.

Of Course, She Predicted the Feds Were Going to Pull the Plug.

"She was chosen. She has talent. She has the ability to be a shaman. She is a shaman. She has the gift."

—William J. Cone Jr., attorney for Miss Cleo, the star employee of a $4.99-per-minute psychic hotline that drew fraud complaints from the FTC and nine states. The operation was shut down in November 2002.

1,200 Degrees of Corporate Stupidity

Motivational training . . . team building . . . corporate retreats—doncha just love 'em? Burger King did, until 2001, when a group of BK employees went on a corporate retreat to Key Largo, Florida. The trip was a team-building exercise for the fast-food chain's marketing department, and the highlight of the training was a firewalking exercise. Each of the 100 people in attendance was to walk barefoot across an eight-foot length of hot coals while co-workers cheered. Alas, the corporate ritual didn't have quite the intended effect, unless by "team building" the company meant the bonding of the dozen or so employees who had the first- and second-degree burns on their charbroiled soles treated on-site. One of their co-workers, showing little team spirit, was hospitalized.

"Some people just have incredibly sensitive feet," said Robert Kallen, the motivational coach who organized the fire-walk.

This would be enough, you'd think, to put the fast-food industry off of corporate-mumbo-jumbo retreats forever. But in early 2002, a group of Kentucky Fried Chicken managers found themselves at a similar conference, doing a similar firewalk, with even more casualties: 20 employees were hospitalized with foot burns and 10 more were treated at the scene. One KFC manager said, "We're exploring what went wrong," but just as a precaution, the company banned firewalking adventures at future retreats. Grateful employees would have rushed to thank their bosses, but, well, it's difficult to put much weight on oozing wounds.

So That Explains the "Giant Sucking Sound" Obsession

"They were looking for a sucker."

—H. Ross Perot, explaining why he was hand-picked to salvage the Wall Street brokerage firm duPont Glore Forgan in 1970. The firm collapsed in 1974, forcing Perot to take a loss of $60 million.

So Next Year It's "Take Marisa to the Unemployment Office Day," Got It? Now Hand Over the Key to the Men's Room and Leave.

Bill Means, an engineering manager at Ohio-based Structural Dynamics Research Corp., was looking forward to the morning of April 27, 1995. It was Take Our Daughters to Work Day, and Means was bringing his eight-year-old daughter, Marisa, along to learn all about life in a corporate setting. The paper shuffling! The lines at the fax machine! The mail cart!

The security escort from the building.

That morning, Means was called in by his supervisor and informed that, in a round of layoffs, he was being fired after two years on the job. A guard accompanied Means and his child out of the building. As Daddy struggled to explain what had happened that day, the phone kept ringing with calls from reporters dying to explore his humiliation. Means wasn't keen. The comment from a VP at Structural Dynamics reflected another part of modern life that Marisa had better wise up about: the apology that sounds more regretful about the result than the action. "We're so sorry about this that I don't know how I could express it," said Ed Neenan, who lowered the boom on Means. "It's just made us look like very bad people out here."

And One Day, I'll Get Paid $500 an Hour to Do It!

"I'm busy doing jack shit."

—Jonas L. Blank, in a June 2003 e-mail revealing the dirty little secret of summer law internships. A "summer associate" at the New York law firm Skadden, Arps, Slate, Meagher & Flom, Blank accidentally distributed the personal message to the entire firm.

How to Piss Away 60,000 Bucks in One Night

A recession is a time-honored excuse for a good stiff drink. And if you can close a big deal despite the rough economic weather, more power to you. So it's hard to blame six investment bankers from Barclays Capital in London for heading off to a ritzy restaurant in July 2001 to celebrate a successful round of trading. Heck, the Petrus restaurant manager contributed to the evening's celebratory spirit by picking up the $600 dinner tab.

The wine bill was another matter.

The sextet started modestly, with some juice, 10 bottles of water and a $2,000 bottle of 1984 Montrachet, an esteemed dry white. The stuff must have gone to their heads quickly. The guys proceeded to splash their way through three bottles of World War II–era reds from Chateau Petrus, six glasses of champagne, a couple of bottles of beer and a pack of smokes, presumably for palate cleansing. Closing off the evening, they opted for a bottle of dessert wine—Chateau d'Yquem, 1900. The grand total for the night of imbibing: $62,679 (tip included).

The Barclays bankers received high marks from oenologists for their sophisticated selections when the media got wind of the Petrus pig-out and ran with the story, inaccurately reporting that the bankers submitted part of the bill as a business expense. But at Barclays, where a round of belt tightening was in progress, the affair did not go over well. Eight months and reams of unflattering publicity later (funny how those newspaper corrections columns don't ever really fix much), five of the Barclays six were fired; the sixth was spared because he was a recent hire. Still, Dayananda Kumar, one of the sacked bankers, showed the robust confidence of an especially plucky cabernet sauvignon. "To be honest, I'm not that bothered. I've been on lots of expeditions since I left the bank. I went climbing on Kilimanjaro and I'm off to the North Pole soon," Kumar said—apparently under the impression that the Mackenzie Shelf refers to a collection of fine whiskeys.

CHAPTER THREE

MANUFACTURING AND PRODUCTION

[
Sometimes the idea is fine—brilliant, even—but the execution is just, well, pathetic. Or at least that's how to play it if the nuts-and-bolts guys aren't around to defend themselves.
]

Says You. Personally, We Love a Challenge.

"NOT TO BE USED WHILE DRIVING"

—Warning label for the Express Desk, a $39.95 device from Mobile Office Enterprise that allows users to attach a laptop to the steering wheel of their car

It's a Mysterious Chemical Cocktail, Granted. But We're Sure It's Safe for Babies.

In the late 1970s, Beech-Nut was the second-largest maker of baby food in the United States, but found that the costs of manufacturing its 100 percent apple juice were rising alarmingly. So the company signed an agreement with a new supplier offering an "apple juice concentrate" that in fact included very little in the way of apple-related material. The concoction was mainly water, sugar and chemicals. Since "laboratory sludge" doesn't show up in Dr. Spock as an essential infant nutrient, Beech-Nut continued to reassure parents that its product contained "100% pure fruit juice." Yeah, yeah, it was cheating, but what were the babies going to do? Talk?

The scheme meant big savings for Beech-Nut—$4.2 million in three years—but a concerned chemist at the company felt he should alert his higher-ups about the problem. Hearing nothing back, he sent another note—this time to the FDA. The letter, signed by one "Johnny Appleseed," led to a federal investigation in 1986. The following year, the company pled guilty to 215 felony counts and paid $2.2 million in fines. An additional $7.5 million went to settle a class-action suit, and two executives were sentenced to prison terms.

But the real damage occurred to Beech-Nut's revenues line. Babies can't read, but their parents can. The company's market share dropped from 19 to 15 percent, and losses in 1988 totaled $15 million. Gerber, knowing a good opportunity when it saw one, broadcast ads in the wake of the apple-juice scam boasting that *its* products met or exceeded government standards. Delicious.

Oh, That? That's Just Our Competitive Advantage. Here, Help Me Drag It to the Dumpster Out Back.

You're a venerable company. Beloved, even. Your product has been a global success for generations, and in that time you've learned a lot about manufacturing, distribution and quality control. With this knowledge, you can approach outsourced manufacturing with either

> a. Scrupulous concern about the future health of your company
>
> b. Devil-may-care indifference

Schwinn chose "b." Twice.

In 1981, the famed bicycle company was already speeding downhill with faulty brakes. Neglecting to capitalize on the emerging mountain-bike craze and focusing on wimpy-looking 10-speed bikes instead, Schwinn was also suffering from the effects of a strike at one of its manufacturing plants. Desperate, Schwinn raced to the Giant Manufacturing Co. in Taiwan to handle the majority of its bike production. In the process, Schwinn handed over everything it knew about its business, from technology to production methods to quality control. This not only gave Giant an opportunity to do brisk business making 700,000 Schwinn bikes each year, it also gave the company a chance to improve on the Schwinn design. Making its own line of bikes for sale in the United States, Giant became

Schwinn's biggest competitor. By 1990, Giant was the world's leading maker of carbon fiber–framed bikes.

Most companies, at this point, would have realized the error of their ways. But Schwinn subscribed to the philosophy that if you fall off a bicycle, it's important to get right back up on the bike and fall off again. Looking for a cheaper supplier, Schwinn in 1987 approached a Chinese firm, Chinese Bicycles Co., whose executives proved to be just as bright as Giant's. Three years later, Chinese Bicycles was selling bikes in the United States under the Diamond Back name.

Realizing that it's impossible to fight a two-front war—especially when you helped arm the enemy—Schwinn filed for bankruptcy in 1992. That same month, the president of Taiwan's Giant Manufacturing Co., Antony Lo, offered a eulogy at a bicycle trade show. "Without Schwinn, we would never have grown to where we are today," Lo said. "We learned many basic things from them: quality, value, service." And what not to do when getting into bed with potential competitors.

Platinum? Too Pricey. Silver? Tarnishes. Wait—I've Got It!
Stainless steel. It works for kitchen knives. Why not cars?

In the early 1970s, John DeLorean sensed that he was simply too cool for boring old General Motors. He was the successful head of the company's Pontiac and Chevrolet divisions, but his long hair and flashy lifestyle helped hasten his departure from GM in '73. No matter. He had a plan for a sports car that was going to knock everybody's socks off. Convincing the British government to sink $130 million into his venture, he built a new factory in Northern Ireland and began work on the car. After numerous production delays, the DeLorean was finally introduced in 1981 with a sticker price of $25,000—a lot of dough for a car back then.

The DeLorean had two main selling points: the stainless steel construction and doors that opened by flipping upward. Too bad the flashy gull-wing doors were hard to close from inside the car. And the problem with stainless steel is that it's damned heavy. Ostensibly a sports car, the lumbering DeLorean had a top speed of 75 miles per hour and went from zero to 60 in about 10 seconds—closer to your uncle's Pontiac than a Porsche.

By 1982, DeLorean's dream was going bust; his company was $50 million in debt after manufacturing only 8,500 cars. Worse still, DeLorean was arrested that same year on drug trafficking charges, supposedly for running cocaine to finance his foundering firm. Now, there's an idea. The charges were later dropped when DeLorean successfully claimed he was entrapped by the FBI, but the episode made him an auto-industry pariah (pity he wasn't in the movie business). In 1999, he filed for personal bankruptcy after falling $20 million in debt. At last report, however, DeLorean was back in the stainless steel gadget game, selling $3,500 wristwatches.

Santa Was Wearing a *Red* Suit in *Miracle on 34th Street*? Who Would've Guessed!

Sometimes manufacturing isn't about making anything so much as remaking it. At great cost. And regardless of whether anybody wants it or not. Ask Ted Turner. In the mid-1980s, the media mogul looked at his recently acquired MGM archive of more than 3,000 movies and did *not* revel in the glories of classic black-and-white filmmaking, or the subtle interplay of shadow and light, or the emphasis on snappy dialogue over the flash of special effects. Turner's reaction: Who needs that crap?

Besides, market research indicated that TV viewers switched channels as soon they encountered black-and-white programming. So Turner started "colorizing" the movies at the rate of two a month, spurring a brief flowering of businesses—including Color Systems Technology, Colorization Inc. and American Film Technologies—specializing in the painstaking colorization process. It was costly, too: upward of $3,000 to tint one minute of film. Even then, the results were unspectacular at best. Colorized faces tended to look jaundiced, feverish or downright radioactive, but rarely an improvement on their B&W pallor. The complaints about the quality of the retouched films—and the wisdom of doing it in the first place—eventually reached the Senate floor. There Ginger Rogers bemoaned being "painted up like a birthday cake" in *43rd Street*; Woody Allen called the process "sinful." (This, of course, was back when Woody Allen could talk about morality without cracking everybody up.)

But the overwhelming expense of giving Jimmy Stewart & Co. a makeover eventually landed the colorizing firms in a tub of red ink. By the end of the decade, Color Systems Technology, the first company to colorize movies, was $19 million in debt; Colorization Inc. filed for bankruptcy; American Film Technologies saw its profits steadily decrease and moved into animation.

Early on in the colorization minicraze, Turner defended the practice by saying that they were his movies and, he added, "I can do what I want with them." And so he did. In 1994, he launched Turner Classic Movies, a cable channel that broadcasts old movies in their lovely, original black and white.

The Undrinkable Swill That Made Milwaukee Infamous

For those who missed it the first time around, a brief primer of the Beer Wars of the Nixon era: In the early 1970s, Anheuser-Busch and Schlitz were battling for market share. Anheuser-Busch tried to win by promoting fresh ingredients, high quality and spare-no-expense production methods. Schlitz, apparently, drank too much of its own product.

Schlitz had recently been taken over by Robert Uihlein, who had no experience in the brewing industry but knew how to read marketing research, which told him that in taste tests, most people couldn't differentiate between beer brands. So in 1974, Uihlein launched a thorough cost-cutting initiative. Barley malt would be replaced with cheap corn syrup. Hops were replaced with "hop pellets." Fermentation, which usually took 12 days, would now take only four. To keep Schlitz on the shelves longer, the company introduced a distressing-sounding en-

zyme substitute it called "Chill-garde," which theoretically pre-
served the beer for as close to eternity as possible. Oh, and
Schlitz raised its prices.

Of course, none of this was presented as a cost-cutting
move. Schlitz promoted its dubious new production techniques
as something called "automated balance fermentation."

Chill-garde, however, did creepy things to beer, creating
small white flakes that made you wonder if the bartender who
just served up that tall, cold stein of Schlitz ought to switch to
a dandruff shampoo. Not using barley cut costs, but barley is
what puts heads on beers. Schlitz tried to explain that its de-
capitated beer didn't taste any different, but guys in bars tend
to shoot their mouths off, and slowly word got around that
Schlitz was pushing an inferior product.

Schlitz's market share tumbled. By 1980, sales were down
from 24 million barrels yearly to 15 million barrels. Distributors
sued, and by 1985, Schlitz was a subsidiary of Stroh Brewery
and had only one percent of the beer market. Today Schlitz is
owned by Pabst, which describes the brew as "the classic
American Beer with a brewing tradition going back more than
a century." The Chill-garde tradition, thankfully, has been put
on ice.

The Regina Monologues

In the late 1980s, it looked like vacuum cleaner manufacturer
Regina was cleaning up big time. In 1986, the company reported 300 percent profit growth, and in 1988, it excitedly told
investors to "look forward to some significant new announce-
ments."

Indictments on fraud charges probably wasn't what Regina meant.

The company's CEO at the time, Donald Sheelan, had mortgaged most of his personal assets when he purchased Regina and was looking for a quick way to boost profits. Cutting manufacturing costs seemed like a smart move. Regina began experimenting with replacing metal parts in its vacuums with plastic. The company's R&D department was told to ignore the pages of their engineering texts that explained how plastic is more prone to melt at high temperatures than metal.

Nature may abhor a vacuum, but that was nothing compared to the reaction of Regina's customers. Complaints about vacuum breakdowns, freeze-ups and failures soared; the company's warehouse ran out of room to store returned product. Unsold inventories skyrocketed, and Regina earned a reputation for execrable quality.

Management did its best to sweep the problems under the rug. In cahoots with CFO Vincent Golden, Sheelan reported artificially high profits to help bolster Regina's stock price. Its 1988 report boasted earnings of $10.9 million. But closer scrutiny of the numbers revealed an internal meltdown. The masses of broken Regina vacuums that were returned weren't deducted from sales; revenue figures were falsified; sales invoices were backdated or completely made up. By 1989, the company reported a $16.8 million loss and filed for Chapter 11 bankruptcy, and two Regina executives resigned and turned themselves in to authorities. Sheelan and Golden were both fined and sentenced to short terms at halfway houses. Whether they were assigned vacuuming duty is lost to history.

Like *The Birth of a Nation*, but with Wacky Neighbors and a Laugh Track

Slavery and the Lincoln White House. What could be funnier?

In 1998, in the midst of complaints that minorities were underrepresented on television, the UPN network weighed in with its attempt to address the issue: *The Secret Diary of Desmond Pfeiffer*, a Civil War–era sitcom whose title character was Abraham Lincoln's black butler. Honest Abe was portrayed as a gay bumbler; First Lady Mary Todd Lincoln, as a crazed nymphomaniac. In one episode, the president engaged in "telegraph sex"; in another, Pfeiffer was chastised by a staffer, who tells him, "The slaves haven't been emancipated yet. Get your feet off the table." Mused Abe during one poignant moment: "I pray I'm doing the right thing, but it feels so wrong that young boys are dying every day on the battlefield—young boys with large biceps and tight washboard stomachs."

Protests inevitably flared, charging the network with racism. But the complaints died down as quickly as it became apparent that *Desmond Pfeiffer* wasn't so much racist as utterly moronic. Lasting a mere four episodes, it ranked 133rd out of 135 shows that fall. A month after the premiere, UPN pulled the plug.

But the network couldn't resist getting in one last Lincoln joke. The next year, UPN entertainment chief Dean Valentine, wearing a stovepipe hat, spoke before critics: "Fourscore and 15 days ago," he said, the network launched a show "dedicated to the proposition that a show about the Lincoln White House could be funny. We were wrong."

You Can't Be Too Careful About the Contracts You Sign. Especially When You're Signing Contracts with Guys Who Are Starting the Long Slide into Becoming Creepy, Obsessively Germ-O-Phobic, Ex–Movie Moguls with Extremely Long Fingernails.

In the early 1950s, airplane manufacturer Convair was attempting to compete with Boeing and Douglas in the commercial jet market. Believing its new Model 880 could help build enthusiasm for medium-range jets, Convair aimed its pitch at Howard Hughes, then the owner of Trans World Airlines. In 1956, TWA ordered 30 of the planes but stipulated in its contract that Convair deal exclusively with TWA.

Unfortunately, Hughes had also put in a $400 million order for a fleet of Boeing jets that same year, which left him scrambling for cash. Creditors demanded a share of TWA for their investment, which Hughes refused to give. Instead of concentrating on curing his financial situation, Hughes devoted his attention to meddling with the 880's design. He turned it into a clunky, slow plane far from the sleek midrange jet that Convair had envisioned. In the meantime, Boeing had unveiled its own midrange jet, the 720, which effectively scotched Convair's line. Convair lost $425 million on the 880 (aka "the flying Edsel") and its uninspiring successor, the 990. Hughes was forced out by TWA's board in 1960; he died in Houston 16 years and gallons of his own stockpiled urine later.

Needless to Say, They Didn't Get the Account for James Earl Carter's Nobel Peace Prize.

"Thank you James Earl Ray for keeping the dream alive."

—From a plaque, created by Texas-based Merit Industries, intended for actor James Earl Jones at an event honoring famous black Americans. James Earl Ray was Martin Luther King Jr.'s assassin.

E.T. Phones It In.

In the summer of 1982, America fell in love with a squat brown creature with leathery skin who could communicate across galaxies with a Speak 'N' Spell. As Steven Spielberg's *E.T. The Extra-Terrestrial* kept busy breaking box-office records, merchandisers scrambled to cash in. Videogame maker Atari ponied up a reported $21 million for the rights to make an *E.T.*-themed videogame. One catch: in order to get the game to market in time for Christmas, Atari had a mere five weeks to produce it.

Once it hit stores, Atari's E.T. Phone Home immediately acquired a reputation—which lasts to this day—as the worst videogame ever made. The object was to move a greenish squiggle (supposedly a representation of E.T. himself) back and forth across the screen while trying to avoid falling into deadly tar pits—which came up so often that the thing was essentially unplayable. In other words, it was a lot like Pong, only less stylish, less technologically advanced and less fun.

E.T. Phone Home was apparently the flagship for what could have passed for Atari's new mantra in the early 1980s: "Crappier games, made faster." Assuming massive demand that never materialized, Atari cranked out Phone Home cartridges as well as those for its similarly mediocre Pac-Man game. As mountains of unsold cartridges were dumped on Atari's doorstep, its parent company, Warner Communications, lost $538.6 million. A large number, yes. Especially in comparison with $240 million—the price for which Warner unloaded Atari in 1984.

Special Bonus E.T.-Related Dumb Moment: The decision by the Mars candy company not to let Spielberg use M&M's as the intergalactic gnome's sweet of choice, thereby ensuring that the much less popular Reese's Pieces—made by the competition over at Hershey—would scarf up pieces of their business.

Special Bonus Atari-Related Dumb Moment: *"Get your feet off my desk, get out of here, you stink and we're not going to buy your product."*
—Joe Keenan, president of Atari, to Apple founders Steve Jobs and Steve Wozniak, in 1976. The two Steves were offering Atari licensing rights for their new personal computer.

Yugo, as in "You Go Call a Tow Truck, We'll Stay Here Being Heckled by Passing Motorists."

No matter how many millions of dollars he loses, no matter how appalled reviewers are by the cars he tries to sell in America, no matter how eager consumers are to chase him with a hatchet, Malcolm Bricklin is going to be an auto magnate some day. He's been trying for more than 30 years. Oh, there was that Subaru minicar he introduced to the United States in 1968, a safety-free vehicle that *Consumer Reports* warned "shouldn't be accepted as a gift." Perhaps stung by the criticism, Bricklin in the early 1970s manufactured his own car, the Bricklin SV-1, the "SV" standing for "Safety Vehicle." With its frequently inoperable gull-wing doors, the eponymous Bricklin might have made owners wish they owned a pony instead. Bricklin declared bankruptcy in 1975 after the project lost $32 million.

Bricklin completed the crap-car hat trick in the mid-1980s, when he decided that what America really needed was one of Europe's worst automobiles. He pitched Yugoslavian auto manufacturer Zavodi Crvena Zastava on the idea of bringing its subcompact Yugo to these shores. Bricklin managed to persuade 170 dealerships to take on the Yugo. The price was right. At $3,990, it was a full thousand bucks cheaper than any other car then on the market.

But, whether you're using dinars or dollars, you get what you pay for. Based on a 25-year-old Fiat design, the Yugo sustained the most damage of any car at speeds of five miles per hour, according to one test; another determined that front-seat occupants would likely die in any head-on collision of 35 miles per hour or more. One analyst noted its "vague transmission." *Consumer Reports* found 21 flaws, including oil leaks and a faulty ignition switch, and suggested drivers invest in a good used car instead. J. D. Power & Associates proclaimed the Yugo "the worst car in America."

"It's a good machine," Bricklin insisted. But in 1992, after years of recalls and complaints, Yugo of America went bankrupt, having fallen $30 million in the red.

Bricklin's true talent may be in persuading investors to part with their money. In the 1990s, his smaller-and-cheesier-is-better transportation philosophy had been whittled down to producing an electric bicycle; the EV Warrior went down to defeat in 1997. But by 2002, Bricklin was reviving the idea that something good and automotive was just bound to come out of Eastern Europe. He was plotting with Serbian manufacturers to import an inexpensive latter-day Yugo in the form of the ZMW (Zastava Motor Works). Somehow, we doubt we'll ever hear the words *Hey, nice Zeemer.*

And a Helluva Lot More Interesting to Watch, Too
"It would have been cheaper to lower the Atlantic."
—British film producer Lord Grade, on production costs of the 1980 film *Raise the Titanic,* which grossed $7 million in the United States against a budget of $36 million

My, the Fashion-Conscious Well-to-Do Sure Are Chucking a Lot of Contaminated Blood Samples This Week.
In the go-go 1980s, Neiman Marcus figured that it could sell anything—*anything*—so long as it had that "designer" cachet. So in 1987, just in time for the Christmas season, the retailer introduced a line of designer garbage bags. Like any couture product, the bags didn't come cheap—$6.25 for a box of 20— but Neiman Marcus knew what it was selling: snobbery so thorough that it extended right down to the disposal of coffee grounds and orange rinds. "We've taken the utilitarian trash bag and elevated it," said a spokesperson, about to make per-

haps the first garbage-related pun in the company's history, "to a hefty art form."

Sure, why not? Heck, when the paté is past the sell-by date, the rich—or at least the help—have to toss it just like anybody else cleaning out the fridge. One problem: the company had made the bags a cheeky "jungle red"—to coordinate with the maid's lipstick, perhaps. In the waste-hauling business, however, the color red signifies hazardous or infectious waste, so sanitation workers refused to pick them up. It was a vexing development for its cosseted customers, but Neiman Marcus soothed their concerns by bringing out a spring 1988 line of bags in "subtle paradise jade."

CHAPTER FOUR

SENIOR MANAGEMENT

> What's the difference between a business and a fish?
> Both rot from the head, but a rotten fish head can't
> squander investors' fortunes, speak total drivel for
> public consumption or be led away in handcuffs.

**Plus, He Had His Head, Connected to His Neck, Stuck Up
His Own Butt, and You Could Still Hear Him.**

*"I had jets with my engines hit a building I insured, which was
covered by a network I own, and we still grew earnings by 11
percent."*

—General Electric CEO Jeffrey Immelt, explaining that his company
weathered the September 11 terrorist attacks quite nicely, thank you

Jamie, You Were Supposed to Run This Quote Past Corporate Communications, Not Jeffrey Immelt.

"The most patriotic thing we can do is make money."
—Jamie Karson, CEO of shoemaker Steve Madden Inc., explaining why no proceeds from sales of an American-flag-themed shoe made after September 11, 2001, went to firefighters' charities, despite earlier promises. After reporters revealed the problem, the company pledged 10 percent for charity.

Good Thing He Was So Decent and Honorable. Otherwise, He Probably Would Have Thrown in a Few Hookers and a Couple Kilos of Coke.

Some companies, like some children, are slow learners. In 1977, Congress passed the Foreign Corrupt Practices Act (FCPA), which was inspired in part by the questionable activities of airplane giant Lockheed earlier in the decade. The company had been in desperation mode at that point. Production of its L-1011 TriStar was botched when the jet-engine manufacturer, Rolls-Royce, went bankrupt. Lockheed would eventually lose $2.5 billion in the debacle, which helps explain why the company, eager to move whatever TriStars it could, started greasing more than just jet turbines. Lockheed doled out bribes left and right, from a million bucks for a Dutch prince to $14 million slipped to Japanese officials. All told, Lockheed spent $22 million in airplane payola, leading to the resignation of several company executives, some noisy political theater and eventually the FCPA.

Undeterred, Lockheed returned to its grafty ways in the 1980s. At a meeting to negotiate a deal to sell three cargo jets worth $79 million to the Egyptian government, Lockheed execs approved a $1 million under-the-table payoff. In 1995, Lockheed fessed up to the payola and agreed to pay a $24.8 million penalty, the maximum FCPA fine that could be levied at the time. One executive resigned in the scandal. Another, Suleiman Nassar, attempted to flee to Syria; he was later caught and sentenced to 18 months in prison. "I apologize for what happened," he told a federal judge. "I really think I'm a very decent and honorable man."

A *Stupid* Stand Would've Cost Twice as Much.

"It's not just some stupid dog umbrella stand. It's a very unique, beautiful piece."

—Wendy Valliere, interior designer for indicted Tyco CEO Dennis Kozlowski, in 2002, describing the $15,000 antique Kozlowski allegedly charged to the company. Valliere also consulted on the purchase of a $6,300 sewing basket, a $2,200 wastebasket and a $445 pincushion.

But at Least He Had the Presence of Mind to Snag a Few Cases of Heidelbergs on His Way Out the Door.

"DON'T SUFFER IN SILENCE," bellowed an ad in the pages of the 1900 Sears & Roebuck catalog. Decades before Viagra was the source of the gleam in Bob Dole's eye, men plagued with virility troubles sought scientific help—and pseudoscientists were glad to oblige. Hence, Sears's "Heidelberg Electric Belt," a contraption that looked like a high-voltage jockstrap and promised a battery-powered romantic assist, as well as curing rheumatism, sciatica, liver disorders and—oh, what the hell— "almost every known disease and weakness."

Though the electric snake oil sold for $18 apiece, the company claimed that only three customers had ever taken them up on the money-back guarantee (a safe claim, since complainers would invite the supposition that they had such a tenacious case of impotence that even genito-electroshock therapy couldn't cure it). At the turn of the century, company founder Richard Sears, a huckster at heart, was just as happy selling patent medicines and cheap gewgaws—including "pink pills for pale people" and $1.95 "Stradivarius" violins— as more useful items like pocket watches and overalls. But his recently added partner, Julius Rosenwald, thought Sears's approach would eventually earn the company a tawdry reputation. And so eight years of bitter in-fighting ensued, prompting Sears not only to quit in anger, which was understandable, but also to sell off all his stock in the company he started, which was nuts.

Rosenwald became one of the richest men on the planet as the company turned into the country's largest catalog retailer, a distinction it held until 1990. Richard Sears died in 1914 with nothing to pass along to his heirs.

Sears's original partner, Alvah Roebuck, had sold his interest in 1900, claiming health concerns ("Sears—get away from me with that belt!"). Roebuck, who made off with a mere $25,000, had no regrets. "Sears made millions and he's dead," Roebuck said in 1938, when he was 74. "Rosenwald made one hundred million dollars and he's dead. Now look at me. Haven't been sick in twenty-seven years." He lived on for another decade.

Oh, Michael. You Know How They Are. Jealous That a Prime Cut of Beefcake Like You Wouldn't Take the Oath of Ooooomerta.

"It was the goal of these people to eliminate me. . . . They wanted to kill Michael Ovitz. If they could have taken my wife and kids, they would have."

—Ex–Walt Disney Company president and former despotic supremo of the Creative Artists Agency Michael Ovitz, in a 2002 *Vanity Fair* interview, explaining that "they" were a dastardly "gay mafia." Ovitz later apologized.

We Never Did Figure Out the Whole Jon Peters–Peter Guber–Pete Peters–Jon Guber Thing. And Then They Were Gone.

In the late 1980s, Sony started shopping for a movie studio, dreaming of synergies with its music and electronics divisions. Columbia Pictures, which the Coca-Cola company had purchased for $752 million in 1982, was on the block. After years of trying to manage a money-losing studio, Coke sensibly realized that the making and selling of carbonated beverages was still its true calling. Sony, less sensibly, paid $3.4 billion—also known as 22 times the studio's cash flow—to buy Columbia, and then put a couple of Hollywood producers, Peter Guber and Jon Peters, in charge.

A minor detail—the fact that G&P were under contract to Warner Bros.—turned out to be a big deal, costing Sony an additional $600 million just to liberate them and officially bring the pair to Columbia. In the meantime, the duo began a massive $100 million renovation of the studio itself (the sort of project that entailed planting trees around the lot, realizing they didn't look impressive enough, ripping them out and replacing them with bigger specimens). Over five years, Sony sank $1 billion into Columbia.

For all this, Sony got a steady stream of cinematic mediocrities, including *Radio Flyer*, *City Slickers 2*, *I'll Do Anything*, the $80 million *Last Action Hero*, and *Gladiator*—no, not the Oscar-winning instant classic starring Russell Crowe, but the instantly forgettable 1992 version with Brian Dennehy.

In 1994, both Guber and Peters were shown the door—with a $200 million golden handshake for the pair as a lovely parting gift. At the end of the year, the company announced a $2.7 billion write-off on its film ventures and a $510 million operating loss.

But Sony assured investors that after the Guber-Peters debacle, everything was going to be fine. After all, the studio was hard at work on *Jumanji* and a remake of *Godzilla*.

Lie Lady Lay

"Everything we had was mostly in Enron stock. . . . We are struggling for liquidity."

—Linda Lay, Enron chairman Kenneth Lay's wife, tearfully explaining her low station on NBC's *Today* show in January 2002. In fact, the Lays held $8 million in other corporate stock and $25 million in real estate.

Absolutely Fatuous

Ernst Malmsten and Kajsa Leander were hip. They had youth, designer clothes, fashion eyewear and rich pals. In 1998, as dotcom delirium raged, they also had a lot of money. With $135 million of venture capital, they began building Boo.com, a fashion Web site that Malmsten promised would be a "gateway to world cool."

Malmsten was right—but it seemed like there was only room in the gateway for him and his business partner. They took $150,000 annual salaries; they also doled out $100,000 allowances to themselves for London apartments and another $100,000 in decorating costs. They spent more than $650,000 on promotional gewgaws, $600,000 for a PR firm and $42 million on a global ad campaign.

Apparently lost in the shuffle was the main reason they received the venture-capital bounty in the first place: to build a Web site that would sell fashionable clothing online. Boo.com was initially slated to launch in June 1999, but the site's construction was beset with errors, technical glitches and endless fussbudgeting over the look of "Miss Boo," the site's mascot. When Boo.com finally did launch in November, many of the technical problems remained, leading Federated Department Stores to pull its planned $10 million investment.

By April 2001, Boo.com was taking in just $1.1 million a month, which barely covered massage costs for Boo's hundreds of employees working in New York, London, Paris and Stockholm. If there was a city packed with insufferable eurotrash, Boo was there, but customers were hard to come by.

On May 17, 2000, Boo.com shut down for good and sold its assets for $2 million. Later, when reporters suggested that the founders spent their venture capital too extravagantly, Leander bristled. "I only flew Concorde three times," she said, "and they were all special offers."

We Never Figured the Quaker Oats Guy for a Leg Man.

"There was so much excitement about bringing in a new brand, a brand with legs. We should have had a few people arguing the 'no side' of the evaluation."

—Former Quaker Oats CEO William Smithburg, ruefully discussing his company's $1.7 billion purchase of Snapple in 1994. The "no side" might have argued, for instance, that Snapple deliveries required a fleet of refrigerated trucks, which Quaker didn't happen to own. The company sold Snapple after three years, taking a $1.1 billion loss.

Don't Telegram Us—We'll Telegram You.

"Guitar groups are on the way out," one record executive in the early 1960s announced as he declined to sign up the Beatles. It's a dumb-business tradition: seeing your ship come in and waving from the pier as it slowly sails away. Nobody, though, did it better than Western Union.

In 1876, Alexander Graham Bell was understandably proud. As the inventor of the telephone, Bell figured he was on the ground floor of something big, though he wasn't sure how big. He'd already been memorably shot down once by no less than the president of the United States. "An amazing invention," Rutherford B. Hayes observed, "but who would ever want to use one?"

Not having much of a head for business, Bell solicited his father-in-law, Gardiner Hubbard, to look into ways of profiting from the device. Hubbard's first stop was Western Union, which was such an obvious choice, as the developer of the telephone, that Thomas Watson, Bell's assistant, later confessed that he was entertaining "visions of a sumptuous office" at the company's headquarters. Hubbard pitched his deal to Western Union president William Orton: for $100,000, he could own the patents to Bell's device. If they'd been on the phone, Orton would have hung up on him—this "electronic toy," he said, wasn't of interest to a communications colossus like Western Union.

Hubbard slunk away and started his own company. Thirty-one years later, American Telephone and Telegraph had the pleasure of buying Western Union. Which would seem to be the end of the story, except that 100 years later, the two companies aren't together anymore. And as cell-phone users stagger around trying to find a signal and shouting "You're breaking up," you can almost hear the ghost of Rutherford B. Hayes cackling through the dead air.

Why Mass Transit Has Such a Hard Time Succeeding in This Country

"[W]hat you are doing, as managers, with this company makes me SICK. . . . I know the parking lot is not a great measurement for 'effort.' I know that 'results' is what counts, not 'effort.' But I am through with the debate. . . . Folks, this is a management problem, not an EMPLOYEE problem. Congratulations, you are management. You have the responsibility for our EMPLOYEES. I will hold you accountable. You have allowed this to get to this state. You have two weeks. Tick, tock."

—Neal Patterson, CEO of software company Cerner, in a March 2001 e-mail to management staff. Patterson was concerned with the emptiness of the company parking lot, while investors, after the e-mail was leaked, became concerned about the stability of Cerner and Patterson himself. The company's stock sank 22 percent in the three days after the e-mail leaked.

In a Time of Great Struggle . . . in a World That Wouldn't Listen . . . One Man . . . Will Stand Alone: Boss Kevin Costner in Three (Mis)Steps.

1. Having already scored big by turning Boomer boyhood fantasies into multimillion-dollar projects (Get to be a baseball player in *Bull Durham*! Dress up like a Native American in *Dances With Wolves*! Play Robin Hood in . . . you get the idea), Costner in 1994 produces and stars in another classic of young-male wish fulfillment, *Wyatt Earp*, a three-hours-plus dissection of the Clanton-Earp contretemps at the OK Corral in 1881. Budgeted at $63 million, *Earp* earns a less-than-OK $25

million in its summer release, prompting *Variety* to dub the Western one of the worst film flops ever.

2. Costner realizes the problem with *Earp*: though he produced and starred, he didn't direct. The trouble is, he doesn't come to the realization until his movie the following year, an aquatic epic about the search for dry land on an Earth flooded by melting ice caps, is nearly finished. When *Waterworld* director Kevin Reynolds quits (can't imagine why), his star takes the helm. The final budget of $175 million, a Hollywood record at the time, suggests that Costner attempted to melt the North Pole itself. Despite featuring at least one landmark moment in film history—the only time a former depictor of Eliot Ness has ever been seen quaffing his own urine on-screen—*Waterworld* makes only $88 million in U.S. box offices. Thanks to video sales and foreign distribution, the movie eventually turns a wee profit, but Costner is pegged by critics and filmgoers as insufferably, ponderously self-absorbed even by Hollywood standards.

3. Costner realizes the problem with *Waterworld*: too much water. His next epic (after a break to play some golf in *Tin Cup*) is set in an arid, postapocalyptic wasteland where the movie's producer-director-star, playing an ersatz mailman, leads a band of rebels offering a special delivery . . . of justice. Audiences in 1997 guffaw at the trailer, which showcases Costner heroically astride his trusty steed and wearing a U.S. Postal Service uniform—so much for the action figure licensing bonanza—leading Warner Bros. to remove most of the mail-carrying imagery on posters and trailers for a movie called *The Postman*. Budgeted at $80 million and featuring inspiring dialogue such

as "It takes one postman to make someone else a postman," the movie posted less than $20 million in U.S. box offices.

There's a Reason Why *Waterworld* Was Called "Heaven's Lake."

United Artists thought it was signing up a prestige picture when the studio greenlighted a historical heartland epic in 1978. Michael Cimino, fresh off Best Director and Best Picture Academy Awards for *The Deer Hunter*, was contracted to make a $7.5 million movie that would take a little more than two months to shoot and run at about two and a half hours. Instead, the *Heaven's Gate* production costs more than quadrupled to $36 million—unthinkably lavish in those days—as the filming dragged on through retake after retake for four months, and Cimino just couldn't bring himself to brutalize his creation by cutting the movie to less than five and a half hours. Nervous UA envoys who ventured to the set in Montana to find out what the heck was going on were greeted by auteur hauteur; the studio didn't clamp down until the blown budget threatened to sink United Artists itself.

Critics able to peer through on-screen dust storms detected a terrible movie, and audiences in 1980 simply stayed away from what the *New York Times* termed "an unqualified disaster." *Heaven's* box-office gate was hellish—the first weekend pulled in just $1.3 million. A year later, United Artists' owner, Transamerica, sold off the damaged studio. Cimino became the poster boy for the dangers of indulging visionary directors, which is why today all creative decision making in Hollywood is entrusted to CPAs. But Cimino wasn't drummed entirely out of the business. His 1996 film, *The Sunchaser*, starring Woody Harrelson, wrapped filming three days ahead of schedule and under budget. The movie opened in only about two dozen theaters, taking in what *Variety* described as a "gloomy" $609 per screen its opening weekend.

Even Better: The Fetus Is in an Airtight Compartment, so There's No Danger of Secondhand Smoke. Fire 'Em Up, Ladies!

"Some women would prefer having smaller babies."
—Joseph Cullman, then chairman of cigarette manufacturer Philip Morris, after being presented in 1971 with studies showing the correlation between pregnant smokers and low-birth-weight babies

Oh, C'mon, That Joe Cullman Quote Was from Three Decades Ago. Cigarette Makers Have Become Much More Socially Responsible Since Then.

"At some point they will learn to crawl, and then walk."
—RJR Nabisco chairman Charles Harper, at a shareholders meeting in

April 1996, explaining that infants who have a problem with secondhand smoke can just move to another room

And They Say It's Impossible to Foul Yourself.

The American Basketball Association of the 1970s seems like a long-lost era of professional basketball utterly unconnected to today's National Basketball Association. Gone are the red-white-and-blue basketballs, hot-pants uniforms, Afros the size of beanbag chairs and entire rosters of players who'd never been handcuffed and shoved into the backseat of a patrol car. But vestiges of the ABA do survive, in the form of four teams that joined the NBA—and the spectacularly terrible deal their owners struck with the ABA's St. Louis Spirits in order to free themselves up to make the switch. When the ABA folded in 1976, the NBA absorbed the Indiana Pacers, the Denver Nuggets, the New York (now New Jersey) Nets and the San Antonio Spurs. Under the rules of the merger, those teams were supposed to arrange compensation for the remaining teams, including the Spirits. Most took what was on offer (the Colonels owner got $3 million) and scuttled away, but Spirits owners Donald Schupnak and brothers Dan and Ozzie Silna held out for a better deal. In the end, the four NBA teams agreed to give the three men $2.2 million plus one-seventh of their annual television income.

In perpetuity. Forever.

It was the smartest deal in sports history, which means somebody at the other end deserves the title for dumbest. In the pre–Michael Jordan era, "TV income" didn't instantly translate as megamillions. For the entire 1980s, in fact, the deal paid the Silnas and Schupnak a relatively modest $8 million. But then 10-figure TV dough started rolling into the league, and every year a good chunk of it—about $13 million at last count—goes straight to the former owners of a team that never dribbled a ball in the NBA. Pacers president Donnie Walsh desperately tried for five years in the 1990s to buy out the deal when it became apparent what sort of bonanza the ex-ABA teams would be shelling out, but finally gave up in 1999. Over the past quarter century, the Silnas and Schupnak have been compensated for their nonexistent troubles an estimated $100 million through the end of the 2001–02 TV contract. Despite his first-class compartment on a long-rolling gravy train, Ozzie Silna does keep busy. Sticking a needle in his reluctant benefactors, Ozzie runs an embroidery company that sells caps emblazoned with the old Spirits logo and the words "In Spirit—In Perpetuity."

CHAPTER FIVE

PUBLIC RELATIONS

[
Let us pay tribute to the artistry that goes into uttering
an explanation-free explanation of brain-locked
malfeasance that might damage a company's relations
with the public while managing to keep a smile
holding firm at 32 degrees Fahrenheit.
]

I'd Like to Teach the World to Spew, in Perfect Harmony. . . .

"It may make you feel sick, but it is not harmful."

—Coca-Cola spokesperson Rob Baskin in June 1999, after contami-
nated Coke products in Europe resulted in a flurry of hospitalizations in
Belgium. The episode led to the largest product recall in the company's
history, $200 million in losses and the resignation of chairman and CEO
M. Douglas Ivester.

. . . I'd Like to Give the World a Coke, and Embarrass the Company.

In May 1990, a bomb squad rushed to San Francisco International Airport to look into a tip from a panicky flight attendant. There was something weird going on with the Coke can she opened during a flight from Chicago; she tried to pour it, but nothing came out. Passengers were hustled off the plane and the can was taken to a remote site. The bomb squad painstakingly scrutinized the can . . . weighed it . . . delicately began to explore its insides . . . and then . . .

Blam! A 10-dollar bill came out.

So ended Coca-Cola's three-week flirtation with sticking foreign objects in its beverages. Dubbed the MagiCan, Coke's prize promotion hid bills of various denominations in selected cans; pick the right one, and a spring-loaded device offered up cash money. To disguise the winning cans, Coke filled them with nonpotable water that winners in theory couldn't get to. But according to the *Wall Street Journal,* during the first week of the promotion an 11-year-old Massachusetts boy "popped open the can and, because of a defect, drank some of the water."

As word of broken MagiCans hit Coke headquarters, the company went into triage mode, placing ads explaining how to spot them. But between the bomb scare, a sick kid and a confused populace—they're not really putting strange objects in my soda, are they?—Coca-Cola canned the promotion.

So *That* Explains the Peculiar General Tso's Chicken They Serve in Amsterdam.

Publicists have a thankless task. How would *you* like to clean up after Courtney Love, say, or Tommy Lee? Then again, the VP of corporate communications at KLM Royal Dutch Airlines probably would have taken one of those jobs in a heartbeat in the spring of 1999, not long after an unusual cargo arrived at Amsterdam's Schipol Airport. Employees at KLM Royal Dutch Airlines were at a loss about what to do with the shipment from Beijing: 440 live squirrels, but no documentation showing they were disease-free. What to do? Send them back? Quarantine them? Call the local humane society for advice?

Nope. KLM's solution: shove those cute li'l nut grubbers into a giant shredder.

The fur *really* started flying when news of the mass rodenticide surfaced. It turned out that KLM had been operating the shredder for years, using it to dispose of live turtles, birds—any errant fauna that came the company's way. KLM apologized and said it would consult with a local squirrel refuge for future squirrel-handling advice. But it was a moot point. A few months later, KLM announced that it would no longer accept shipments of amphibians, reptiles, endangered animals—or, for that matter, squirrels.

Sure, Sure, the Customer Is Always Right. But What If the So-Called Customer Hasn't Actually Entered the Store Yet?

In his autobiography, *Made in America*, Wal-Mart founder Sam Walton described the three pillars that make a great company:

respect for the individual, service to customers and a strive for excellence. On a quiet evening in Illinois in 2002, all three pillars got knocked down impressively in less than a half hour.

Heading into the Wal-Mart in Geneseo to pick up a prescription, a 73-year-old woman stopped to buy a newspaper from a box outside the store. As the woman removed her paper and turned away, the door slammed shut on the drooping hood of her jacket. Unable to wriggle out of the garment thanks to recent shoulder surgery, the septuagenarian looked around for assistance. A young woman spotted her predicament and went into the store to find a helpful Wal-Mart employee. Respect for the individual was on its way!

Alas, the woman was informed that Wal-Mart had a strict policy against tampering with newspaper boxes.

With the woman still held hostage by the Quad Cities' *Dispatch/Argus*, a Wal-Mart employee, mindful of the all-important service to the customer, called the paper to have someone sent over to liberate her.

The woman politely suggested that the employee simply cough up the two quarters and open the damn door.

This concept wasn't found anywhere in Walton's book or the employee handbook. The store, she explained, didn't offer refunds for the newspaper.

Fifteen minutes passed. No sign of a *Dispatch/Argus* rescue squad. Desperate, the senior citizen laid out the plan again: two quarters, placed one after the other into the newspaper box, would result in the unlocking of the door, which would enable her to be freed. Fifty cents . . . door . . . freedom. It had a crazy kind of logic! Throwing corporate guidelines to the wind, the employee tried the coin solution and—bingo!—another member of the greatest generation was sent toddling down the sidewalk.

The woman's grateful daughter later came to the store and entrusted a five-dollar bill to the Wal-Mart employee, for use solely to underwrite future pedestrian releases. It was proof that when people work together to strive for excellence, everybody wins. Sam Walton would've been proud.

Where's the Wal-Mart Newspaper Box Detention Center When You Need It?

You're a greeter at a Wal-Mart outside of Oklahoma City. A man walks up to you wielding an ax. Do you:

  a. Stall as best you can while discreetly signaling for someone to call the cops?
  b. Gently suggest that the man leave the ax in his car?
  c. Put a sticker on the ax so that other Wal-Mart staffers know that it's his ax and not Wal-Mart's?

The greeter, in the storied spirit of Wal-Mart's fine customer service, chose "c."

Alas, on Independence Day 2001, Wright Barnard Raynor celebrated his freedom to wreak havoc. He'd stolen the ax from a nearby Home Depot, which he proceeded to rob; used the ax to threaten employees at a convenience store, which he also robbed; and then gone to the Wal-Mart, which he robbed as well. After crashing his (stolen) pickup truck in Arkansas, Raynor was finally apprehended. A Wal-Mart spokesperson contended that the greeter had made an understandable mistake, since the guy's weapon didn't look as menacing as reports had indicated: "It was a hatchet, not an ax."

Turns Out That When They Charge You $6 for a Cup of Warm Bud, They're Actually Doing You a *Favor.*

Butts in seats. Owners of professional sports teams say it all the time: "You gotta get butts in the seats to make money." Pro sports teams, needless to say, have perfected a number of wacky ways to accomplish just that, from $1 million half-court shot contests to bring-your-pet-to-the-park day. Generally speaking, the more desperate the team's situation, the more over-the-top the promotion.

Which brings us to the 1974 Cleveland Indians, who were spending their fifth straight season at the bottom of the AL East standings. Only about 8,000 fans would file into Cleveland's Municipal Stadium every night to keep a bedside vigil. Then management came up with a breakthrough promotion: the June 4 game against the Texas Rangers would be 10-cent-beer night.

Cheap beer does indeed get butts in seats—when they're not standing in line outside the men's room. Attendance more than tripled, to over 25,000. But it turns out that you really don't want to concentrate thousands of drunks in one place and give them three hours to kill. Reporters in the press box could hear fireworks being set off in the first inning. In the second, a woman flashed the crowd from the on-deck circle. Mooners, streakers and empty beer cups started populating the field, as did scarier stuff: rocks, golf balls, batteries. By the seventh inning, the Rangers wisely moved their bullpen to the safety of the dugout.

Then, in the ninth inning, a fan, apparently overcome with an urge to help the Indians as they rallied to tie the game 5–5, ran onto the field and stole Rangers outfielder Jeff Burroughs's glove. Burroughs gave chase but soon found himself swarmed by wobbly, hostile Cleveland fans pouring onto the field. Billy Martin—who, startlingly, wasn't at the concession stand with a roll of dimes but rather was the Rangers manager at the time—grabbed a bat and ran onto the field to protect his player. A massive melee ensued, giving the outfield an aroma of blood, beer and sweat that at least freshened the scent usually wafting over from nearby Lake Erie. Umpire Nestor Chylak, despite being whacked over the head with a chair, kept his senses long enough to declare a forfeit and award the game to the Rangers.

Dime Beer? Hell, If We Promise to Set Off a Bomb, We Can Charge Full Price for the Brew!

What is it about the Great Lakes area that turned Major League Baseball games in the 1970s into public relations nightmares?

In 1979, Michael Veeck was a frustrated rock-and-roll gui-

tarist living in a disco nation. But rather than trade in his ax for a drum machine, Veeck decided to take a public stand for rock and roll—or at least against disco. It helped that his dad, Bill Veeck, as owner of the Chicago White Sox, had access to the rather large stage of Comiskey Park and that the senior Veeck was extremely receptive to goofball ideas. Bill, after all, had signed up midget Eddie Gaedel for the St. Louis Browns in 1951 to create both the smallest strike zone and tackiest stunt in baseball history. So it was the work of a moment for Michael to convince his dad that it would be deeply cool to blow up a bunch of disco records at a baseball game.

And so, on July 12, 1979, the Sox held an antidisco "Demolition Night" and promoted a 98-cent admission for anybody who arrived for a Sox-Tigers doubleheader with a disco record in hand. The vinyl would be placed in a Dumpster and destroyed with a quarter stick of dynamite between the games. Local radio DJs Steve Dahl and Garry Meier, who routinely held antidisco rallies, agreed to preside over the event.

As the first game plodded on, the fans grew impatient

and—understandably intrigued by the aerodynamic possibilities of tossing a record across an outdoor amphitheater instead of a living room—started winging their Gloria Gaynor and Village People sides from the upper deck. One player wisely donned a helmet in the outfield. The first game ended with the lowly Sox losing, 4–1. The prospect of management-sponsored violence and destruction stoked the sense of impending anarchy, but the event proceeded as planned, or at least as scheduled: the disco-Dumpster detonated, which 2,000 wild-eyed fans took as a signal to spill onto the field, run the bases, dance on disco debris, spin records through the air at eye level and play tag with a few humorless, hard-charging cops. At one delirious point, play-by-play announcer Harry Caray tried to soothe the rioters by bellowing his customary rendition of "Take Me Out to the Ballgame" over the loudspeakers.

The umpires, surveying the mayhem and vinyl shrapnel on the field, called off the game. The next day, a forfeit was declared, with the Tigers getting the win.

That Said, We're Still Going to Keep Our Factories Open. Setting aside hacking coughs, tumors, tracheotomies, yellow teeth, heart disease, lung cancer, mouth cancer, throat cancer, low birth weight, emphysema, wrinkles, general respiratory disorders and the potential for untimely death, combined with the related heartbreak it causes to your family and loved ones, smoking has its benefits. In 2001, Philip Morris distributed a report in the Czech Republic arguing that, in 1999, smokers saved the Czech government $30 million in health care and other costs by performing the kindness of dying early. Once word of the report leaked out, the company fashioned a quick apology, saying that the study it commissioned was "not just a terrible mistake. It was wrong. All of us at Philip Morris, no matter where we work, are extremely sorry for this. No one benefits from the very real, serious and significant diseases caused by smoking."

If You Don't Have Anything Nice to Say, Why Not Wear It on an Adorable Little T-shirt?

"We poke fun at everybody, from women to flight attendants to baggage handlers, to football coaches, to Irish Americans to snow skiers. There's really no group we haven't teased."

—Hampton Carney, spokesperson for clothier Abercrombie & Fitch, explaining the company's line of Asian-themed T-shirts reading "Wok and Bowl," "Get Your Buddha on the Floor" and "Wong Brothers Laundry Service—Two Wongs Can Make It White." The company recalled the shirts less than two weeks after putting them on sale in April 2002.

Find the Moment When Financial Analysis Became Wall Street PR.

"Stock prices have reached a permanently high plateau."

—Yale professor and stock analyst Irving Fisher, in September 1929, mere weeks before Black Monday

"The end of the decline of the stock market will probably not be long—only a few more days at most."

—Fisher on November 17, 1929, after the stock market lost $20 billion

"For the immediate future at least, the outlook is bright."

—Fisher, going down with the ship, in 1930

And If Something Went Wrong with the Screen While They Were Showing *The Birth of a Nation*, Somebody Always Had a White Sheet Handy.

In countless ways, American society has improved over the past century. For instance, you no longer need the Ku Klux Klan as customers to help make your film a success. In 1915, D. W. Griffith released his brilliant and disturbing *The Birth of a Nation*, a tale of the Klan's rise during Reconstruction. The film was a huge hit, even though moviegoers took whatever message they liked from it. Thanks to *The Birth of a Nation*, the ranks of the KKK swelled.

Wounded by charges of racism, Griffith was determined to demonstrate with his next project that he was a decent person. Unfortunately, he wasn't much of a businessman. Griffith took most of the $400,000 he earned from *Nation* to make *Intolerance*, an epic film about the scourge of bigotry. Juggling four plot lines, ranging from the days of ancient Babylon to contemporary America, Griffith spent lavishly on sets, including a massive 140-foot-high wall that loomed over Hollywood. With a cast of thousands, a three-hour running time and a then-astronomical production cost of $2.5 million, *Intolerance* was released to the utter bafflement of audiences, who apparently didn't consider tutorials about Huguenots in Paris as their idea of a good time. *Intolerance* met with box-office indifference.

Film scholars later embraced the movie, but Griffith never completely recovered as a filmmaker. After losing his independent studio, Biograph, in the wake of the disaster, he was forced to make small films with smaller budgets. He died in 1948, but *Intolerance* has a way of popping up from time to time. The Babylonian set was a Hollywood tourist attraction years after the film's release, and the fiery destruction of Griffith's studio in 1962 had a certain epic poignancy. And in 2002, building developers opened Babylon Court, part of the sprawling Hollywood & Highland shopping and entertainment complex. Guarding the entrance: two 30-foot-high elephants—reproductions from Griffith's grand, failed effort at spin control.

Silly Ash

"I'm just sorry that so many young people will be exposed to it. I'm terribly upset to be presented in such a disrespectful way."
—Bill Ripken, then second baseman for the Baltimore Orioles, discussing his 1989 Fleer baseball card, which featured him holding a bat with the words "fuck face" on the knob, written in felt pen by a practical-joking teammate. The Fleer card company apologized to the Orioles and hastened to cover up the words in later pressings. The collectors market soon bid the card above $100; these days, Ripken cards featuring the obscenity sell for about fifty bucks.

Chuck Berry's Customer Service Rule No. 1. Or Was It No. 2?

Chuck Berry has brought us many memorable phrases. Johnny B. Goode "could play a guitar just like a-ringin' a bell"; "Maybellene, why can't you be true?"; "Roll over Beethoven, and tell Tchaikovsky the news." But maybe the most telling line he ever uttered was "What's moral to one man might be a little bit immoral to another." And it wasn't even a lyric.

Now, a certain amount of turpitude comes with the musical territory. Berry spent two years in jail in the early 1960s for

violating the Mann Act by transporting a minor across state lines for immoral purposes, but, then, Jerry Lee Lewis and Elvis Presley liked 'em young, too. Berry, a notorious cheapskate, has also had trouble with the Internal Revenue Service; maybe he was using Willie Nelson's accountant.

But Berry's scatological obsession might make even the seediest rockers think twice about sharing guitar picks with him. It certainly wasn't good for his restaurant business.

The musician's Southern Aire restaurant in Wentzville, Missouri, near St. Louis, offered more than just down-home cooking to its female patrons in the 1980s. They got the chance to star, unwittingly, in toilet-cam videos shot by the proprietor. Berry's secret potty setup wasn't flushed out into the open until 1989, when a former cook sued him for invasion of privacy. The Southern Aire promptly went out of business. By the following year, 74 women had filed a class-action suit against Berry as friends and customers complained that he had surreptitiously taped them undressing and using the bathrooms at the restaurant and on other property Berry owned. Although he denied any involvement with the taping, in 1995 after much legal wrangling, Berry agreed to pay a $1.2 million settlement. No telling how many former patrons still get the creeps when they hear "Brown-Eyed Handsome Man" on the radio and wonder what those brown eyes saw.

Our Pledge to You, the Viewers of *Dateline*: From Now On We'll Pretty Much Stick to Stories About Sex.

On November 17, 1992, *Dateline NBC* was doing what network news magazines do best: scaring the bejeezus out of America with a story about another popular product that could kill *you* and *your children*. Consumer advocates had been questioning the fuel-tank safety of some of General Motors pickup trucks when NBC News decided to investigate the matter itself by conducting its own crash test.

Guess what? The results were *terrifying*. The collision! The flames! Of course, it would have been even more remarkable if the test truck *hadn't* self-immolated—it was a Molotov cocktail on wheels. *Dateline* had enlisted a trial-lawyers' advocacy group to help run the test, which was then thoroughly rigged in a way that only a trial lawyer could love: the truck's gas tank was overfilled and plugged with a nonstandard gas cap all but guaranteed to pop off in a collision. Nice touches, of course, but the *pièce de* rig*sistance* was the concealment of remote-controlled model rockets on the truck frame to ensure that the gas-spewing vehicle blew up real good.

The smoldering wreckage on the test site was nothing compared to the damage sustained by NBC News's reputation when GM found out about the ruse and went public. The carmaker also shifted its NBC News advertising to sports and entertainment, threatened to cancel all of its ad spending on the network, and sued NBC for defamation. The suit was resolved when NBC aired an apology in February 1993 and agreed to cover the $1 million cost of GM's own investigation into the matter. Michael Gartner, NBC's news chief, resigned amid the furor and moved to Iowa to run a newspaper chain. "Everybody wanted blood," he told a reporter. "I thought I would just offer up mine."

The WB Network Will Be Hearing from the Yeats Estate Shortly.

"The name referred to a guy's name with specific personality traits that the public through media publications had come to associate with me—irreverent, aggressive, unapologetically male, smart, and contemporary."

—Filmmaker Spike Lee, in legal papers, claiming that The National Network president Albie Hecht had publicly used similar words to explain the cable channel's planned name change to Spike TV; Lee sued to stop the move. In an interview about the name choice, Hecht did indeed cite Lee—along with director Spike Jonze, a character in Buffy the Vampire Slayer and the volleyball maneuver. After three weeks of sniping, TNN parent Viacom and Lee reached a settlement of undisclosed terms. But observers noted that when the judge ordered him to put up a $2.5 million bond to cover Viacom's damages if he lost, in addition to the $500,000 bond he already had on the line, Lee appeared to become a lot less aggressive. But don't get us wrong—he was still plenty irreverent, unapologetically male, smart and contemporary.

For Sale: New Car, Used

One evening in 1986, two Chrysler execs decided to take a car fresh off the assembly line in St. Louis out for a spin. They must have gotten a little carried away, because a police car soon pulled them over. The cop asked the inevitable question—"Do you know how fast you were going?"—but didn't get the usual response: *No, officer. See, we've disconnected the speedometer and odometer.*

The officer could have written a ticket on the spot for driving without a cerebrum. For trying to avoid the price of a speeding ticket, the duo ended up costing Chrysler millions. One of the perks of being a Chrysler executive, a little police investigating soon revealed, was that you occasionally got to take the new models out for a test drive. Check the steering. Step on the brakes. Fiddle with the odometer so nobody notices that the car was aired out with a 400-mile joyride before being shipped to the dealership as brand new.

The practice had been in place since 1949, and it took nearly 40 years before the company got caught. Charged with 16 counts of fraud in 1987—investigators said about 40,000 cars were involved—Chrysler initially denied the allegations. But in midsummer, chairman Lee Iacocca acknowledged the tampering:

> The first thing was just dumb—we test-drove a small percentage of our cars with the odometers disengaged and didn't tell our customers. The second thing, I think, went beyond dumb, and reached all the way out to stupid—a few cars were damaged in test-

ing badly enough that they should never have been sold as new.

Chrysler continued to deny any *illegal* activity, but reaching all the way out to stupid still has its costs: that December, the company agreed to shell out $16.4 million to 39,000 buyers of the "new" Chrysler cars.

Why, I Stepped on a Dead Otter on the Patio Just This Morning.

"There are natural seeps all over this country. Oil in the water is a phenomenon that has gone on for eons."
—Exxon executive Don Cornett, in 1989, explaining to an Alaskan community why the nearby *Exxon Valdez* oil spill was just the ecosystem going about its business

Better Adjust Their Meds Over in Customer Relations.

In e-mail programs, "bcc" means "blind carbon copy." People use it when they don't want one recipient to know that someone else received the same message. The "cc," or "carbon copy" option, of course, lets everybody know who's seeing the message. Sounds simple, right? Tell it to Eli Lilly. In June 2001, the pharmaceutical company sent out an announcement that it was discontinuing its Medi-Messenger service—an e-mail sent to Prozac users reminding them to take their dose. Except Lilly made a depressing mistake, also circulating the e-mail addresses of the more than 669 recipients of the message. Lilly seemed to have some sort of Prozac-related psychosis, because the following year the company took a new round of flak when it sent free Prozac samples through snail mail to 300 Florida residents with a history of depression. "We are very excited to offer you a more convenient way to take your antidepressant medication," chirped the attached note introducing Prozac Weekly. Sure, *they* were excited, but more than a few recipients probably went into an emotional tailspin when they realized that a giant pharmaceutical company had been tracking their mental-health status.

The Importance of a .999999-to-.999999 Relationship with Customers

A favorite joke of computer geeks in 1994 went like this: "What's two plus two? 4.000001." Which would, naturally, be greeted with the equally mirthless "LOL."

But even if techies aren't exactly humorists for the ages, they were responding to a laughable gaffe by chip maker Intel that year. When it introduced the Pentium I processor in 1993, Intel made the usual boasts about speed, power and accuracy. In November 1994, though, a Virginia math professor posted a note on the Internet exposing a defect in the chip's calculating abilities in regions well east of the decimal point. It was a rare problem as well—Intel said it was likely to occur once every 27,000 years, which is why it chose not to publicly disclose the problem.

But you know how that darned Internet is. Word got out. Massive overreaction ensued. Intel was deceiving the public! The very integrity of mathematics was being undermined!

Owners of PCs with the slightly flawed chips demanded re-funds and replacements. Computer-industry journalists told readers to delay purchasing Pentium-powered PCs. IBM, in the midst of the holiday shopping season, decided not to ship Pentium-based PCs, whomping Intel's stock.

For a month, Intel insisted that the problem was minor and had no effect on casual users, but less than a week before Christmas, CEO Andy Grove cried uncle. Intel offered to re-place the chip, free of charge.

Intel eventually spent $475 million on chip-replacement surgery, plus $6 million to settle the inevitable lawsuits. For a while, even the slightest flaw in a Pentium chip resulted in a flurry of press releases and groveling public disclosures from the overcompensating company. Eventually, customers came to trust the Pentium, leaving computer geeks free to return to their regularly scheduled quoting from Monty Python skits.

CHAPTER SIX

SALES AND MARKETING

> Selling the product—it's the moment that businesses live for, obsessively grooming and perfecting the message as they put their best foot forward. Funny how often they step in something squishy.

What Were They Doing? Reading Larry King's Mind?

"Where can you find a morning news anchor who is provocative, supersmart and, oh yeah, just a little sexy? CNN. Yeah—CNN."

—CNN—yeah, CNN—taking a sledgehammer to anchor Paula Zahn's credibility as a journalist in a TV ad promoting her show in early 2002. The word *sexy* was accompanied by the sound of a zipper being yanked.

Broncos 34, Falcons 19, Just For Feet 0

Ah, the Super Bowl. On one wintry Sunday, Americans gather in front of their home-entertainment centers to savor corporate America's latest branding initiatives, interspersed with a few palate-cleansing moments of football. In 1999, shoe-store chain Just For Feet was in desperate need of a major image boost. After it took on $43 million in debt from an acquisition that made it the country's second-largest shoe retailer, the company was expanding more slowly than analysts had hoped, and its stock was sinking. So, at a cost of $20 million, Just For Feet launched a new ad campaign, to be introduced during the Super Bowl.

Here's what millions saw: A black Kenyan runner, barefoot, is being tracked by a group of what look like white paramilitaries in a Humvee *(feeling queasy yet?)*. After the men trick him into drinking a knockout drug *(the bathroom's down the hall)*, the runner collapses *(we'll wait here)*, and his captors force a pair of Nikes on his feet. As the runner comes to, he spies the shoes and screams in protest *(tum-de-dum-de-dum)*.

When critics held the company's Just-For-Feet to the fire, chairman and founder Harold Ruttenberg scrapped the $3 million ad a week after its debut. Unwilling to leave bad enough alone, though, the company took the novel position that it had nothing to do with its own advertising and in fact had been victimized by the ad's creator, Saatchi & Saatchi. In April 1999, Just For Feet sued Saatchi for malpractice, alleging that the firm "acted recklessly and in willful disregard of professional standards." Just For Feet sought $10 million in damages and refused to pay for the commercial. Although we couldn't find any reports on the outcome of the case, and lawyers for both companies declined to comment, Just For Feet could have used the 10 mil. They filed for bankruptcy seven months later and then sold out to another retailer, Footstar, in 2000. Which is all very interesting, but doesn't answer the question: What the hell was the ad's message? That talented Kenyan runners have to be dragged kicking and screaming into wearing the product the store sells? Smaaaart.

What About "Enough Cargo Space to Transport 12 Adulterous Harlots to the Soccer Stadium for Beheading"?

"It shows that the Taliban are looking for the same qualities as any truck buyer: durabilty and reliability."

—Toyota spokesperson Wade Hoyt, in 2001, explaining the popularity of its Hilux compact pickup truck in Afghanistan

So *That's* How the Rubber Fetish Got Started.

In the 1760s, Englishman James Graham, like so many immigrants before and since, saw America as the land of opportunity. In Graham's case, it was the opportunity to set himself up in Philadelphia as an eye doctor without performing the unprofitable and time-consuming chore of actually getting a medical degree. Also like many newcomers to these shores,

Graham had a restless spirit. Why settle for being a doctor when you could also turn yourself into an electrical engineer? Inspired by word of Benjamin Franklin's electrical experiments, Graham began toying with the stuff himself. Combining his negligible medical knowledge with his scant understanding of electricity, Graham invented what he called "electric therapy," which he argued could cure all sorts of ills.

Graham's true calling, of course, was marketing. Moving back to London in 1770, he converted a residential space into the Temple of Health, hung bawdy paintings on the walls and stocked the place with half-naked women to beckon to prospective patients. Needless to say, visits there weren't covered by Georgian HMOs. But there were lines out the door. Graham might have lectured about the panorama of health benefits offered by "electrical baths" and his "magnetic throne," complete with a wired crown, but the real attraction was the "Celestial Bed," where electricity streamed through a headboard engraved with the phrase "Be fruitful. Multiply and Replenish the Earth."

Graham hoped to replenish his lavish lifestyle by charging the stratospheric price of £50 for the Celestial experience. But after two years, the novelty had worn off, and the supercharged bed wasn't bringing in either couples having trouble in the bedroom or thrill seekers. Graham cut admission prices and moved the Temple to smaller quarters, making it more of a chapel of health. The place featured a couple of new attractions: immortality-ensuring mud baths and gambling tables. That's when the authorities swooped in and shut the place down. Graham's quack-physician, electro-scamming, mud-is-forever rip-off was one thing, but illegal gambling was beyond the pale.

On the Other Hand, Massengill Does Work Wonders on Mildew and Soap Scum.

"Wives often lose the precious air of romance, doctors say, for lack of the intimate daintiness dependent on effective douching. For this, look to reliable Lysol brand disinfectant."
—From a distressing March 1948 print ad for Lysol, which was in fact the country's leading "feminine hygiene" product until the 1960s, when an American Medical Association investigation showed that the doctors supposedly praising Lysol's romance-preserving qualities—and even its contraceptive powers—didn't exist

Is That a Three-Pound Brick in Your Pocket or Are You Just Happy to Be Using a Wildly Expensive Yet Already Obsolete Technology?

A few years back, stand-up comedians finally got tired of jokes about airplane food and found a new target: cell phones. They keep getting smaller! Crazy!

Actually, it's trying to sell the public on a *bigger* cell phone that's crazy.

In the early 1990s, the future of the cell phone technology that prevails today was still an open question. Service coverage, for one thing, was spottier than Charles Bukowski with chicken pox. Which led Motorola to consider a different kind of cell phone concept: instead of land-based relay towers, why not use satellites, which would give phones a truly global reach? In 1991, Motorola founded Iridium, a separate company devoted to pursuing the idea. After seven years and nearly $5 billion in research-and-development costs—launching satellites ain't cheap—the Iridium cell phone was finally unveiled.

Unfortunately, it was about the size and heft of a brick, with a thick antenna—which helps explain why the phone itself wasn't showcased in Iridium ads. "It's huge! It will scare people," said the company's executive director of marketing. "If we had a campaign that featured our product, we'd lose." Worse still, the phone cost about $3,000, and each call cost about seven bucks. Did we mention that the satellite business is expensive?

While Iridium concentrated on building its global satellite phone network, a suddenly robust, land-based cell business gobbled up the company's potential market. Iridium sold only about 10,000 units in its first six months, well below the target. And those users were unamused to learn that they had to take their $3,000 techno-brick outdoors for the privilege of making a $7 call. "Not having a very small phone and not having in-building coverage . . . hurt the concept a lot," said Motorola's then-CEO George Fisher. Yep.

Less than a year after its launch, Iridium filed for bankruptcy. Iridium CEO John Richardson, who may have been hoping to tap into the lecture circuit to boost revenue, gave his assessment: "We're a classic MBA study in how not to introduce a product."

This Ad Is Like . . . Totally Lame.

Marketers constantly fret about how to reach young-adult consumers before their brand preferences are set in stone. But the Gen X era in the early 1990s made advertisers particularly nervous because those media-saturated kids were deeply contemptuous of attempts to manipulate their tastes, and they were wise to every trick in the Madison Avenue playbook. Trying to sell a candy bar—much less an automobile—to this crowd was daunting. That didn't stop Subaru from trying in 1993—and in the process perpetrating one of the lamest efforts in the sorry annals of youth marketing.

The ad for the Subaru Impreza, titled "Kid," opened with a beflanneled youth standing in front of his Impreza, struggling for the words to describe it. "This car is like . . . punk rock!" he gushes, proceeding to explain how the Impreza embodies all the spirit and joy of a punk rock band. Never mind that a car that's just like a punk rock band would be noisy and shiftless and would break up in six months; the guy's excited. Having prompted howls of laughter from its target market—which seemed a bit tetchy about seeing its youthful search for identity reduced to a marketing tool—Subaru backpedaled. The ad, a press release explained, was "widely misinterpreted as our attempt to target Generation X." But there was no misinterpreting the pink slip Subaru gave Wieden + Kennedy, the firm that created the ad, a few months later. The car company, explained a spokesperson, wanted a fresh start to "regain the identity we seem to have lost."

Now, that was something Gen X could relate to.

If Sex Sells, and People Love Kids, Then Our Statutory Rape Campaign Is Going to Be Huge.

Adman William Free first attracted the attention of the National Organization for Women (NOW) in 1970 with his tagline for Silva Thins cigarettes: "Cigarettes are like girls. The best ones are thin and rich." When NOW announced a boycott of the American Tobacco Company smokes, Free—a career copywriter who'd opened the firm F. William Free & Co. the year before—was hardly contrite. He re-emerged with a campaign for National Airlines that brought NOW protesters to his doorstep.

"I'm Cheryl—Fly Me" became National's new slogan in TV and print ads featuring a smiling young stewardess with a come-hither look in her eyes.

But it wasn't this ad that brought out the pickets, or even rival Continental's entry in the lecher sweepstakes, a TV ad that ogled a stewardess from behind as she promised, "I shake my tail for you." Using sex to sell was hardly news even then, and National's campaign worked. The company's first-half revenue for 1972 increased 19 percent, and Cheryl appeared in a new ad celebrating her success, saying, "Millions of people flew me last year." Cheryl then took a break—can't blame the gal—and made way for her replacement in a new round of ads that proclaimed, "I'm Eileen—Fly Me."

Eileen was eight years old.

That's when NOW, bless 'em, went ballistic, thronging

F. William Free & Co. with signs saying, "I'm Bill—Fire Me." Free, who apparently interpreted this as proof he could really attract the ladies, greeted the protesters with roses.

National's success as the class act of the friendly skies wouldn't last. A lengthy machinists' strike in 1974 crippled the company, and in 1980, it was purchased by Pan Am, which itself was grounded 10 years later.

SPECIAL BONUS SECTION
THREE CLASSIC MOMENTS IN BUSINESS DUMBNESS

CLASSIC MOMENT THE FIRST: How Many Dutchmen Does It Take to Screw Themselves in a Tulip-Bulb Mania?

Thanks to the marketing genius of a well-known botanist and an apparently ineradicable chink in human nature, in 17th-century Holland tulips were the equivalent of Hummers and Hermès Birkin bags: inexplicably prized objects that became insanely overpriced. The nascent tulip bubble got its first little puff of air in 1593, when botanist Carolus Clusius arrived in the Netherlands from Vienna bearing tulips he'd received from an ambassador of the Ottoman Empire. Tulips weren't unheard of in Holland before Clusius's arrival, but he was particularly deft at growing the flowers in a variety of intense colors, though a bit stingy about passing them along to enthralled onlookers; he was willing to sell specimens, but only at what he considered prohibitive prices. Fed-up local gardeners soon broke into Clusius's tulip proving grounds at the University of Leiden and absconded with a set of bulbs.

That's when the Dutch went nuts. By the 1630s, market-savvy horticulturists and brokers were selling tulip futures, though the supply of bulbs—which take seven years to mature into something that will bloom into an actual flower—wasn't keeping up with the number of willing investors. One desperate farmer paid for a Viceroy tulip with the makings of a Colonial Williamsburg exhibit: wheat, rye, wine, beer, butter, 1,000 pounds of cheese, a bed, a suit, a silver cup, 4 oxen, 8 swine and 12 sheep. The speculative bubble had grown to immense proportions by 1637, until one anonymous man decided to put the brakes on the ongoing demonstration of the "greater fool" theory, which posits, in economic lingo, that there's always some schmuck who's willing to pay more for an overvalued stock then you did. At an auction in Haarlem, the buyer refused to pay for the bulbs he'd successfully bid on. Instead of setting off a simple eBay-style warning to the populace ("Mr. Voorheldt is a bad buyer! Does not pay!"), the buyer's defiance touched off a panic as the Dutch collectively realized their folly. Tulip prices plummeted, and the Dutch government implemented restrictions on the tulip trade.

All of which, of course, has made tulipmania the pundit's favorite parallel for the Internet bubble of the late 1990s; tulips then, garden.com now. But if scandal stretches across the centuries, so does irony. As of this writing, tulipworld.com, which sells Dutch tulips online, is reportedly alive and well.

CLASSIC MOMENT THE SECOND: All Hail the Utopian Turtletop!

You might think that the problems with the Ford Edsel were its silly name and obnoxious styling—and you'd be right. But more than anything else, the biggest flop in automotive history was an object lesson in bad marketing.

When it came time in 1957 to launch the automobile named after Henry Ford's son, the company decided to play up the car's mystery. Initial ads in *Life* magazine featured a picture of only the hood ornament—which turned out later to have a nasty habit of flying off at high speeds and cracking the windshield. The ad copy simply read "The Edsel is on its Way." Consumers who hadn't been present at the pitch meeting could have been excused for thinking of "Edsel" on the same continuum as Redcoats and plague.

Dealerships were under strict orders to keep their Edsels covered until the official launch date, which succeeded in piquing more curiosity about the car, but Ford neglected a cardinal rule of marketing: If you're going to tease the public, you'd better make the wait pay off. When September 4, 1957, rolled around, thousands of Americans rushed to catch their first glimpse of . . . a gaudy yet homely automobile with a strange push-button transmission, a grille that one wag said looked like a toilet seat and brakes that worked intermittently. Assembly workers, apparently chafing on the Edsel production line, had a habit of shipping cars to dealers without including all the essential parts.

Ford was hoping to sell 200,000 Edsels a year. After three years, fewer than 150,000 were on the road. Ford put the line out of its misery, at a loss of $250 million. There must be a few old-timers in Detroit who still wonder what might have happened if, instead of saddling the car with such an ungainly, nepotistic name, Ford had listened to poet Marianne Moore. In the early going, the company hired the Pulitzer Prize winner to come up with a name that "flashes a dramatically desirable picture in people's minds." Maybe, just maybe, if Ford had taken one of Moore's suggestions, millions of graying Boomers would today fondly recall riding in the backseat of the Utopian Turtletop, the Pastelogram or the Mongoose Civique . . . or maybe not.

CLASSIC MOMENT THE THIRD: Like Our Product? Then You'll Love Our Ill-Conceived Reformulation of It!

Market research. It tells you what your customers care about. It suggests what products you should consider for the future. Then again, it also begets New Coke.

In the early 1980s, Sergio Zyman had every reason to be cocky. As the head of marketing for the world's largest cola company, he had presided over successful introductions of Diet Coke and the "Coke Is It" ad campaign. The man with the golden cola touch was chosen to head up a bold new venture: fiddling with the name and recipe of the company's 99-year-old flagship product. Research indicated that not only did the slightly sweeter Pepsi regularly beat Coke in tens of thousands of blind taste tests, but a more sugary version of Coke also stomped on the traditional formula. No wonder, then, that in a generally stagnant cola market, the leader, Coke, had been steadily losing share to Pepsi for 15 years. But taste wasn't the only issue. It was also about perception. The two competitors' images seemed to be: Pepsi young, Coke old.

Hmm, how to make Coke seem not-old? How about renaming it . . . New Coke? And lace it with more sugar to make the young'uns happy!

On April 23, 1985, after four years of planning, Coca-Cola yanked its venerable namesake and unveiled New Coke to the nation. Unfortunately, the company hadn't taken into account another aspect of public perception: Americans felt attached to Coke in a way that went well beyond simple product identification. And the springtime launch gave them plenty of time to bellyache at barbecues, picnics and Little League games about the cavalier desecration of an American institution. The company's Atlanta headquarters was besieged with 1,500 angry phone calls daily. Pundits had a field day. A beleaguered spokesperson insisted, "It's a smoother, rounder taste. We say 'Try it.'"

To which the country replied, "We say, try to make us." Coke shipments fell 15 percent the following month, and the clamor for the traditional version of the world's most famous carbonated beverage continued. On July 11, the company caved, announcing the return of the original Coke, rechristened Coca-Cola Classic. To this day, Zyman (who resigned and was later rehired) and Coca-Cola insist that the episode ultimately was good for the company because it made consumers realize their strong attachment to the Coke brand. Kinda like the way people weep with gratitude when a family member who has been taken hostage is released unharmed.

THIS ENDS THE SPECIAL BONUS SECTION. WE MAKE NO CLAIMS REGARDING THE LONG-TERM SIGNIFICANCE OF THE ITEMS THAT FOLLOW.

Thus Bringing New Meaning to the Term *Slush Fund*

New Coke wasn't the only bit of lunacy Coca-Cola has committed in the fog of cola wars. In 2000, the company decided that Frozen Coke, a slushy beverage sold in Burger King restaurants, was an underexploited product. The company urged BK to spring for national promotion, but the restaurant chain balked, insisting on a two-week test in Richmond, Virginia, where customers would be given a coupon for a free Frozen Coke with the purchase of a "Value Meal" sandwich–fries–drink combo. Fair enough. But when initial sales from the promotion tanked, Coca-Cola—forever looking madly over its shoulder at PepsiCo's creeping advances—couldn't just drop the idea. The company frantically tried to put the fix in, giving $9,000 to a marketing consultant with instructions to make some value-meal sales happen. He trotted off to several boys and girls clubs in Richmond, where the inner-city youngsters were given this life lesson: *Guess what? There is such a thing as a free lunch when hitting corporate target sales is involved.* Burger King was sufficiently impressed by the end of the trial that it spent about $10 million for a national campaign.

So far, so devious—but not dumb, unless Coca-Cola got caught. It took three years, but word finally leaked out in 2003 when an ex-employee from Coke's auditing department contended in court that he was fired for being the internal whistle-blower who exposed the marketing department's antics in

Virginia. The company didn't contest Matthew Whitley's story, but simply dismissed it by saying that BK had been offering Frozen Cokes in a majority of its restaurants since 1999, so the undercover shoperation was only a silly mistake. In other words, Coca-Cola was duping Burger King just for the hell of It.

The fast-food giant was irate, but then, in August 2003, the two warring parties announced a truce. Why the BK change of heart? Possibly it was the $21 million in reparations Coca-Cola offered to the company and its franchisees. Otherwise, we're stumped. Coke also smoothed out things with Whitley, reaching a $540,000 settlement in October 2003. But you can't throw money at the feds to make them happy. At last report, fraud investigations by the Justice Department and Securities and Exchange Commission continued.

Worse, Herb Was Later Spotted at a McDonald's— on a Date!

Sometimes, as with the Frozen Coke stunt, it's an outsider yanking Burger King around. At other times, the fast-food chain yanks itself. In 1985, anticipating a 10 percent increase in its market share, BK launched a $40 million ad campaign that regaled America with the story of Herb, a guy who—*are you ready for this?*—had never, ever eaten a Whopper. After months of teaser ads, the nation finally got a look at Herb during the 1986 Super Bowl.

America collectively shrugged, despite the company's dangling a $5,000 prize for the first person to spot Herb at a Burger King restaurant. Sales crept up only 1 percent. That was disappointing, but perhaps more damaging was the impact on

101

the brand: rather than associating BK with tasty, inexpensive food, the Herb project cast the company as one that liked to ridicule folks who dress badly, look homely and no doubt constitute a sizable part of the burger-buying public.

Jingle Writing: A Complex Art Form

"Get your girl in the mood quicker / Get your jimmy thicker / With St. Ides malt liquor."

—Ice Cube, rapping in a 1996 radio ad for St. Ides malt liquor. It was pulled after complaints from inner-city community groups.

One Man's Vandalism Is Another's Weak Attempt at Guerrilla Marketing.

San Francisco sidewalks are chock-full of unusual characters: drag queens, hippies, former dotcom CEOs holding up signs saying, "WILL ENGINEER IPO FOR FOOD." In April 2001, IBM decided that what the city really needed was more penguins. To promote its new line of Linux-enabled workstations, IBM "street teams" began covering the sidewalks with stenciled images of a peace sign, a heart and an image of Pokey the Penguin, the open-source operating system's mascot. Talk about street cred! Plus, the campaign was harmless—after all, they were just using biodegradable chalk. Er, make that spray paint. San Francisco cleaning crews clocked 200 hours trying to rid the town of the tenacious but otherwise entirely ineffective icons. IBM paid the city $100,000 for its part in making the botched marketing effort go away.

Hacking Our Way to Victory: Five Camel Cigarette Ads from the World War II Era

1. SOLDIER ONE: "Right now I feel the urge for a Camel!" SOLDIER TWO: "That's the old Army spirit. Camel's the smoke with us."

2. "In this man's Navy, it's Camels. What flavor!"

3. "There's an added pleasure in giving Camels at Christmas. . . . So remember those lads in uniform."

4. "He's a bombardier. He's the business man of this B-17E bomber crew. . . . But when those 'office hours' are over—well, just look below and watch him enjoying a Camel."

5. "Hide-and-seek. A deadly game of it with the TNT of depth charge and torpedo. That's a game only for steady nerves. But, then, what isn't these days—with all of us fighting, working, living at the highest tempo in years? Yes, and smoking, too— perhaps even more than you used to."

Kraft Singles. Or Was It an Error?

Buy cheese, win a minivan. That was the essence of Kraft Foods' Ready to Roll game in 1989, which challenged contestants to match one half of a prize image included in Kraft Singles cheese with halves included in newspaper ad circulars. The grand prize: a Dodge Caravan. Forget about the "challenged" business; instead of printing a solitary van-winning image, as planned, the company accidentally put 10,000 of them into circulation. Kraft pulled the emergency brake on the minivan game after discovering the error, but it still had to confront thousands of angry customers. Two years and one class-action lawsuit later, Kraft finally settled the matter, offering payouts of nearly $600 in cash and $150 in Kraft coupons to the non-van-winners. All told, Kraft spent $10 million making amends. "If the game had operated correctly," a Kraft spokesperson said, "it would have cost $63,000."

The Suction Specialists Whose Promotional Savvy Blows

News flash to Hoover: people just love to get a good deal on airline tickets. The vacuum-cleaner company's British division apparently was unaware of this fact in 1992, when it struck an alliance with a travel company to award free round-trip airline tickets to folks who bought a certain amount of Hoover products. Now, it might have been an effective promotion if, say, the company got customers to buy enough vacuum-cleaner gear to clean a 40-story apartment building just for the chance to get two cheapie seats from London to Brussels and back. Big purchase, tiny rebate; companies do it all the time.

Hoover's Brits must have inhaled too many shag-carpet fibers in the 1970s, because the company offered two free tickets to a variety of European destinations to customers who spent just $150 on Hoover products. You could go RT from London to New York or Orlando for a $375 outlay. Shoppers did the math and quickly sucked up every Hoover item they could find, cleaning out appliance stores. More than 200,000 qualified for the free rides. The travel agents initially hedged about whether they would make good on the offer, enraging many of Hoover's customers—which isn't exactly the aim of corporate promotions. The company finally came through, setting up a complaint hotline and negotiating a ticket deal with British Airways. The solution might have given the company a clean slate with consumers, but it dirtied up the company's finances. In the first quarter of 1993, Hoover announced a $30 million loss on the promotion. When the dust finally settled, the tab came to $50 million—but at least the company saved a few bucks on the salaries of the three execs it fired for coming up with the plan.

Just Like *The Odyssey*, but Smellier

In the spring of 1987, America fell in love with a fledgling business operation that grew so instantly famous, a day rarely went by that the newspapers or TV news or even Johnny Carson on the *Tonight Show* didn't give it the sort of affectionate attention that marketers dream of. Which would have been great if the product in question hadn't been garbage.

The trash saga began in 1986, when a New York landfill in Islip, Long Island, announced that it was running out of space, which was music to the ears of folks in the hauling business. For trucking the garbage upstate, they could charge a princely $86 a ton—double the cost of using local landfills. They hadn't reckoned on a solution proposed by Lowell Harrelson, an Alabama building contractor with an interest in the hauling business. Harrelson's big idea: why pay absurd rates for trucking the stuff when you could ship it by barge down the coast for just $50 a ton? He'd sign up Southern farmers to let him dump the junk down there; with four barges hauling 10,000 tons of garbage daily, he and his newly recruited partners on Long Island would book $200,000 in profits *daily*. "He said when he first came here this was better than oil," one of the investors later recalled.

Harrelson may have been able to sell Southern farmers on the idea, but local bureaucrats were another matter. Port after port turned away the Mobro 4000, a skow loaded with 3,000 tons of prime New York garbage on the maiden voyage of United Marine Transport Services. After 155 days and 6,000 miles—and countless newspaper inches, minutes of news coverage and Carson jokes—the festering heap finally found a home: Brooklyn, New York, where the trash would be incinerated and sent to . . . the same landfill in Islip, Long Island, where it had started out. "That's one small barge for New York City, one giant bale of garbage for mankind," said the city's sanitation commissioner.

The debacle cost Harrelson and his backers about a million bucks. But they still had assets. By the end of the year a Virginia mail-order firm was offering "Gar-Barge," a sack of trash reputedly from the Mobro 4000 for $10 a pop. The company wouldn't specify exactly how much garbage each sack contained, because nobody wanted to weigh it. A spokesperson explained, "That stuff is nasty."

Wait'll They Get a Load of Our Wok Campaign—Pol Pot Cookin' Up Some Stir-Fry.

In November 1999, commuters in Taipei, Taiwan, were greeted with a new ad for space heaters produced by the German manufacturer DBK. "Declare war on the cold front!" announced the ad, which featured a cartoon of Adolf Hitler, his right arm raised in that familiar salute. On his left arm: an armband with

the DBK logo replacing the Nazi swastika. German and Jewish residents in Taipei expressed doubt that the sign was quite as tasteful as it might have been, and DBK, which hadn't been consulted, wasn't happy about it, either. So K.E. and Kingstone, the Taiwanese company that sold the heaters and created the ads, pulled them down. An unnamed employee explained the mascot selection to the Associated Press: "We decided to use Hitler because as soon as you see him, you think of Germany. It leaves a deep impression."

David Manning of the *Ridgefield Press* Called This Item "Stupendous! The Dumbest Dumbest Moment Ever!"

Critics are a cranky bunch; it's surprisingly easy to find reviewers who hate even the greatest of movies. Bosley Crowther of the *New York Times*, for instance, called *Bonnie and Clyde* "a cheap piece of bald-faced slapstick" shortly after its release. Finding someone who'll love a lousy movie takes a bit more work. Thus you'd think that finding a critic who seems to love nothing but lousy movies would be a difficult task indeed. Well, you'd be wrong.

107

The Dumbest Moments in Business History

Case in point: In the spring of 2001, Sony's Columbia Pictures division released *The Animal,* a movie that featured B-list actor Rob Schneider acting like . . . an animal. The film was generally ridiculed upon its release; *Rolling Stone* said it "reeks like something produced from a squatting position." Sony wisely figured that such a quote wouldn't look good in its promotional ads. Less wisely, in its scramble to find somebody, anybody, who would say something remotely positive, the company dreamed up a reviewer named David Manning. Ostensibly writing for a real newspaper, the *Ridgefield Press* in Connecticut, the fake critic said of *The Animal,* "The producing team of *Big Daddy* has delivered another winner." Not, presumably, from a squatting position.

Manning just couldn't get enough of the masterpieces coming from Sony. He praised Heath Ledger, the lead in *A Knight's Tale,* as "this year's hottest new star!" Both *Vertical Limit* and *Hollow Man* were, in his estimation, "stupendous!" When a *Newsweek* reporter finally discovered Manning's nonexistence, Sony apologized and suspended two employees. In full-disclosure mode, the studio also admitted that a TV ad the previous summer for *The Patriot* wasn't quite what it seemed. The couple seen beaming about Mel Gibson's Revolutionary War saga—"It's a perfect date movie!" says the woman of a film featuring the graphic decapitation of a soldier by a cannonball—turned out to be stooges from Sony's marketing department.

Nine months after news of the ploys broke, Sony paid the state of Connecticut $325,000 in penalties. A Sony spokesperson also promised that nothing like this would happen again. Rob Schneider remains at large and continues to work in the film industry.

CHAPTER SEVEN

ACCOUNTING

When beancounters go bad! If an office manager does something dumb, you get an oversupply of paper clips. When the accountants, or their bosses, make moronic moves, you kiss millions and millions of bucks goodbye.

Also Known as the "Other Than That, Mrs. Lincoln, How Did You Enjoy the Play?" Perspective on Accounting

"The shame of it all is that underlying the debt and the restatement and the alleged fraud is a really great company."
—John Sidgmore, CEO of WorldCom, in July 2002, after the company filed for the largest bankruptcy in history. The company claimed $41 billion in debts and restated results for the previous five quarters, turning a $3.8 billion gain into a $1.2 billion loss.

Which Is Why Today "The Match King" Merely Refers to Some Guy in New Jersey with an Internet Dating Service

As ambitions go, Ivar Kreuger's was both insanely large and remarkably small. He dreamed of becoming the planet's sole manufacturer of matches.

In the 1920s, he was almost there. With factories in 34 countries, Kreuger had a daunting 75 percent market share in the match business, which earned him the title of "The Match King." A Swedish-born engineer, Kreuger used money from American investors to bully his way into new markets. In exchange for low-interest loans to countries crippled by World War I, he demanded a monopoly on match production. Kreuger's monopolistic practices would've been dubious enough even if he hadn't also done a matchless job of inflating his numbers. Shuttling fake profits through 400 shell companies in 35 countries, Kreuger pulled stunts like counterfeiting $142 million in Italian government bonds and routinely falsifying securities documents for collateral on more loans. When one executive suggested he have his books audited, Kreuger recoiled, "Do you think I'm a crook?" The Match King, emperor of the Match Palace, a crook? Heavens, no.

With the advent of the Depression, Kreuger's financing schemes became harder to pull off, which made the existing scams more difficult to conceal. Apparently sensing his house of cards was about to implode, Kreuger shot himself in the heart in 1932 (a dramatic exit, to be sure, but for sheer suicidal-scam-artist bravura, we'll go with publishing tycoon Robert Maxwell's dive off his yacht in 1991). The Swedes, unaware of their native son's epic thievery, lowered flags to half-mast. The *New Statesman* mourned the death of "a very puritan of finance." Then the auditors arrived and discovered the depths of his fraud. Claims against Kreuger's estate ran to $1 billion, or one hell of a lot of matches.

We Hold This Truth to Be Self-evident, That Not All Men Are Equal to Resisting the Temptation to Steal the Government Blind.

The Declaration of Independence might have asserted Americans' unalienable right to the pursuit of happiness, but it raised that knotty question of how you define "happy." It didn't take long after the Revolutionary War for one citizen to make clear that his idea of a good time was cooking the young government's books for his own benefit.

William Duer began his career honorably enough. A member of the Continental Congress, he started out selling supplies to George Washington's army. That earned him a friendship with Alexander Hamilton, which in turn landed him a post as assistant secretary of the Treasury. Chafing at the crimp in his earning power, Duer soon resigned and returned to the private sector. But he kept his contacts within the Department of the Treasury, gleaning information that allowed him to speculate madly. Meanwhile, Hamilton audited Duer's Treasury work and discovered that he'd pilfered $238,000 from a government infrastructure program. As word reached Duer in 1791 that the feds were coming, he tried to drum up some quick cash by spreading word on Wall Street of big mergers involving his business. A speculative bubble formed as money indeed poured in, but within months the bubble collapsed, bankrupting plenty of Duer's investors.

A year later, Duer was in debtors prison (which, in addition to being a holding pen for dumb-business perpetrators, was itself—didn't Dickens mention this somewhere?—a venerable dumb-business institution that prevented debtors from making the money they needed to pay their debts). Hamilton gathered two dozen Wall Street brokers to devise a way to regulate the stock market once and for all. "'Tis time there should be a separation between honest men and knaves," Hamilton wrote, "between respectable Stockholders . . . and mere unprincipled gamblers." Whew—glad they took care of *that*. Hate to think of *knaves* operating on Wall Street.

Mammas, Don't Let Your Babies Grow Up to Be CPAs.
Most of the time, being Willie Nelson is a good thing. There are the devoted fans, the critical acclaim and enough money to hire a full-time hair braider. But in 1990, the IRS came knocking, claiming that the country-music star owed a leathery jaw-dropping $16.7 million in back taxes. By 1991, the revered national musical icon was rebranded as a groveling tax cheat with the late-night TV ad campaign for *Who'll Buy My Memo-*

ries? The IRS Tapes. Twenty-five songs for the low, low price of $19.95, plus $4 for shipping and handling! Call 1-800-IRS-TAPE now! Nelson needed to sell four million of the tapes to settle his IRS bill; after three months, only 200,000 bleary-eyed TV viewers had bought his memories. Luckily for Nelson, the IRS in 1993 agreed to cut its demand to $9 million and Nelson paid off the debt a year later, aided by the proceeds from the settlement of a suit he filed against his accountants at Price Waterhouse. (Now, there's an accounting strategy worth noting.) And so the Outlaw, right with the law at last, could go on the road again—without having the damned IRS always on his mind.

Lesson: If You Don't Care About Your [Expletive] Business, You'll Make No [Expletive] Money.

At the end of the 1960s, railroads were slowly squeaking their way into irrelevance. Americans by the millions had switched their allegiance to travel by car or plane; freight shippers and the postal service were doing more and more of their business with trucks. Anybody could see that it was a perfect time to launch a railroad merger, *railroad merger* being an accountant's euphemism for *train wreck.*

When the Pennsylvania and New York Central railroads morphed into Penn Central in 1968, the idiocy of the merger became apparent almost immediately. One problem: the man in charge, CEO Stuart Saunders, was considerably more interested in real estate investments than in what he wittily called "the fucking railroad." Another: the clash between the wildly different organizational schemes of the Pennsylvania and New York Central. With no intelligent way of integrating the operations, trains were misrouted, bottlenecked and in some cases actually lost; droves of companies simply took their shipping business elsewhere.

Insiders who were already aware of the internal chaos—which was well hidden in public reports—sold off their stock. A year after the merger, Penn Central began unloading Saunders's prized real estate holdings to help keep the railroad rolling. It didn't work. On June 21, 1970—a year when the company would lose $325 million—the railroad officially jumped the tracks, declaring what was then the largest bankruptcy filing in history.

It's Only Money: An AOL Time Warner Merger/Vanishing Value Timeline

January 10, 2000: Internet giant America Online buys media titan Time Warner in a stock deal worth $166 billion, creating what the announcement calls "the world's first fully integrated media and communications company for the Internet Century." AOL chief Steve Case describes it as "a once-in-a-lifetime opportunity." Time Warner head Gerald Levin says, "I look forward to partnering with Steve Case." It is the biggest merger in history, with a that-day combined value of $350 billion. But the value is tied to stock prices, which can fluctuate. AOL stock drops $1.13, closing at $72.62.

December 5, 2001: Levin announces retirement. AOL stock: $34.75.

April 24, 2002: Company posts first-quarter loss of $54.2 billion, the largest quarterly loss in U.S. corporate history. AOL stock: $19.30.

July 18, 2002: Chief Operating Officer Robert Pittman forced out of company. AOL stock: $12.45.

July 25, 2002: The SEC announces investigation of AOL division for questionable accounting practices prior to merger. More investigations will follow. AOL stock: $9.64.

January 13, 2003: Case announces resignation. AOL stock: $15.03.

January 29, 2003: Company acknowledges losing $99 billion in 2002—including $45.5 billion write-down of America Online's value—the largest annual loss in American corporate history. AOL stock: $13.96.

October 13, 2003: World's first fully integrated media and communications company for the Internet century announces it is jettisoning "AOL" from name, reverting to Time Warner Inc. Soon-to-be-renamed-TWX AOL stock: $15.75.

Oops. Lost $1.3 Billion. Destroyed a Venerable Bank. My Bad.

Figuring out how much responsibility to give a young employee can be a tricky business. But as a general rule, giving a largely untested twentysomething trader a free hand in the

Asian markets probably isn't a good idea. Still, Barings Bank (founded: 1762; most famous client: Her Majesty Queen Elizabeth II) thought enough of Nick Leeson to make him the bank's chief trader in Singapore. After all, in 1993, only a year after arriving in Asia, the derivatives whiz raked in 10 percent of Barings' total profits with his seemingly magical skill in the arcane art of betting on how others will bet in currency markets.

In 1994, the 27-year-old Leeson was living lavishly but gambling badly. His hunches, tied to the Nikkei Index, weren't panning out—unbeknownst to Barings. His London bosses had left him in charge of the back office after making him a trader, in effect letting him take positions and settle accounts without any oversight. By the end of the year, Leeson was hiding losses of $512 million. Understandably a tad anxious, Leeson placed a big bet that the Nikkei wouldn't drop below 19,000, only to see the index plummet after the city of Kobe, Japan, was devastated by an earthquake on January 17, 1995. So Leeson did what any freaked-out bettor does: he doubled down. For weeks, he frantically bought up futures contracts on the assumption that the Nikkei would quickly rebound. It didn't. On February 21, 1995—two days before his 28th birthday— Leeson fled his job, leaving a scribbled note on his desk: "I'm sorry." As in, I feel really bad about the $1.3 billion in investors' money that I've secretly vaporized, so I'm going on the lam.

Arrested in Frankfurt, Germany, a little over a week later, Leeson was sentenced to six and a half years in prison for cheating the Singapore exchange and deceiving auditors. About 1,200 Barings employees lost their jobs in the Leeson-ignited debacle, and Barings itself collapsed. The institution that held British royalty's money was purchased in '95 by the Dutch bank ING for the princely sum of £1.

Wow, Stuffing Envelopes at Home Is for Losers!

"Our whole philosophy is based on individual choice."
—AllAdvantage.com CEO James Jorgensen, on the site's plan in 1999 to pay people to surf the Web and use that motivated audience to sell advertising. Using AllAdvantage's proprietary "advertising bar" earned you 53 cents an hour. The company's financial model predicted profitably at 30,000 users. Two million signed up in the first three months, turning AllAdvantage into a classic study in dotcom money-hemorrhaging. In 12 months the company took in $14.4 million, while sending out $49.8 million to its surfing horde on the way to burning through over $100 million in venture capital.

A Long-Term Success, If by "Long-Term" You Mean Four Years and by "Success" You Mean Flirting with Global Financial Catastrophe

Here's the plan: let's start an investment firm stocked to the gills with Nobel Prize–winning economists and other smarty-pants PhD-equipped financial experts, all of them led by John Meriwether, the trading wizard from Salomon Brothers. What team could possibly be more adept at picking sure-fire investments? Answer: maybe the residents of a petting zoo, because the eggheads at Long-Term Capital Management would have been better off buying lottery tickets as investment vehicles.

In September 1998, LTCM threw itself on the mercy of

other financial institutions, admitting that the oh-so-complex computer models designed by partners Myron Scholes and Robert Merton, both Nobel laureates, and their roster of geniuses weren't quite panning out as planned. Fifteen financial institutions ponied up $3.625 billion to rescue the firm, having been convinced that repercussions from LTCM's implosion could wreck the European and Japanese financial markets.

What went wrong? LTCM told its big-ticket investors that its computer models—with Nobel know-how inside!—could anticipate financial movements around the globe. Which was true, at first. In its first three years, LTCM performed spectacularly, building $4.8 billion in equity into a $100 billion behemoth. But the models failed to account for an issue most students learn about in Econ 101: unstable governments tend to lead to unstable financial positions. In August 1998, between Russia devaluing the ruble and defaulting on bonds, and Asian markets falling into a tailspin, investors sold off risky overseas positions en masse. The masse, unfortunately, didn't include LTCM, which rested on its laureates despite being massively invested overseas.

In a matter of weeks, 91 cents of every dollar in the fund was wiped out. Scholes and Merton did what Nobel winners so often do: they came up with a bright idea, fleeing the firm in 1999.

Tell You What. How'd You Like to Get Back _Double_ the Money You Spent on This Book? Just Recruit Four of Your Friends to Buy It and We'll Give Them the Same Deal. Honest.

Runny nose? You reach for a Kleenex. Need something copied? Have it Xeroxed. Busted for operating a pyramid investment scam? You're running a Ponzi scheme.

Around the time of the First World War, Charles Ponzi, an Italian immigrant, marched across North America assembling a rap sheet for small-time scams. In his travels, he clearly learned that people pay more attention to fancy-sounding names than dubious résumés and put that knowledge to use when he opened the Securities and Exchanged Co. in Boston in 1919. Ostensibly in the business of making investments in overseas stamp coupons, Ponzi promised investors a 50 percent return on their money in 45 days—and a 100 percent return for those able to keep their hands off their money for 90 days. (Let's do the math. Scribble, scribble. Scribble. Hey—this guy Ponzi's really onto something. I'm off to the Securities and Exchanged Co.!) Ponzi soon found his office flooded with cash. Literally. Bills were stuffed in desk drawers, closets, wastebaskets and, of course, Ponzi's own pockets.

By May 1920, the "Ponzi Plan" had taken in more than $400,000. A few months later, as the fever was stoked by the sight of early investors indeed doubling their money, his office was receiving $250,000 _a day_. Ponzi scrambled to make pay-offs by roping in new investors, but he could see that the well was running dry. Seeking the largest possible pool of suckers, he tried to go public. But there wasn't much time to talk to underwriters. As the feds closed in, Ponzi ran off to Saratoga Springs with $2 million in a suitcase. A *Boston Post* exposé on Ponzi's scheme ignited a run on his offices, where employees shoved whatever money they had on hand into the arms of angry investors.

Ponzi, who fell $4 million short of repaying his due-diligence-challenged clients, spent four years in prison, where he could pine for the days when total strangers just handed him piles of money and he was free to blow it on gold-handled canes, chauffeurs, tailored suits and diamond-encrusted cigar holders.

Which is to say that Charles Ponzi not only invented the pyramid scheme. He also pioneered bling bling.

CHAPTER EIGHT

LEGAL

Arrests, lawsuits, contracts—sometimes it seems like behind every dumbest moment in business history, there's a lawyer.

But Besides That, All the Fundamentals Looked Rock Solid.

"The customers didn't exist. Their mutual fund shares didn't exist. The funded loans didn't exist. The phony customers' phony pledges of their phony fund shares to buy phony insurance ultimately became numbers on a computer tape, which then printed out phony assets for Equity Funding Corp.'s phony books."

—*The Wall Street Journal*, explaining the details of a scam perpetrated by investment firm Equity Funding Corp. The firm continued its fraud for

10 years before being caught by the feds in 1973. Bilking customers out of $300 million, Equity Funding went bankrupt; a dozen company executives served prison terms.

Welcome to Disney World. Or, as We Like to Think of It, Uncle Walt's Cathedral of Pain.

Disney loves cute animals. A fluffy bunny gets transformed into the adorable Thumper. A deer becomes the sweet-as-can-be Bambi. Chipmunks are turned into the lovable, huggable Chip n' Dale.

Ugly animals, like vultures, get whacked with sticks until they die.

Discovery Island, a zoo at Walt Disney World in Orlando, Florida, began attracting the wrong kind of animal in the late 1980s, when vultures started cruising over the park and eyeing the cuter animals below. Disney worriedly began trapping the carnivorous birds, shoving upward of 20 vultures into cages meant to contain only three. One employee, who apparently took the wrong lesson from *Old Yeller*, beat several of them to death with a stick. Hawks are harder to catch than vultures but equally intrigued by scampering little mammals, which explains why the big birds drew gunfire from Discovery Island. Florida's wildlife authorities eventually came calling, charging Disney with 16 violations of state and federal laws.

Early on, Disney claimed that the situation was just a minor bit of confusion. A spokesperson explained that the vulture deaths resulted from a "misunderstanding of the parameters" of wildlife regulations. Eventually, Disney pled guilty to one misdemeanor charge and paid a $95,000 settlement, which the Florida game commission used to help educate the public about being kind to animals. Even the unmarketable variety.

You Mean the Songs on This Album Were Created by Actual Musicians? Get Me Legal!

Rob Pilatus and Fab Morvan must not have read the job descriptions when they were hired in the late 1980s to be the cool-looking models posing as the pop-star duo Milli Vanilli. Otherwise, why would they insist on actually singing? Must have been the Best New Artist Grammy Award in 1990. Or the fact that the "group" sold 30 million singles and 14 million albums with the featherweight ditties on its debut album. But producer Frank Farian—alarmed at the duo's demand to contribute to a follow-up album—revealed 10 months after the Grammies that the crooners of "Girl You Know It's True" were a bit of lip-synching froth fronting for a handful of studio musicians whom no one would ever mistake for male models. The National Academy of Recording Arts and Sciences yanked the award and chastised the record industry; Pilatus and Morvan publicly apologized and spun a tale of threats, abuse and nefarious dealings.

But the real stupidity took place, as so often happens, in the courtroom. Plaintiffs filed scads of class-action suits. "If somebody doesn't speak out, this thing will go on and on," griped one litigant. "There were a number of 14- and 15-year-olds who got their first taste of deception because of this," a lawyer huffed, apparently referring to teen clients who had yet to uncover the whole Santa Claus scam. The courts finally ruled in 1992 that Milli Vanilli fans were entitled to refunds—more than a year after the lip-stinking farce came to light, and after plenty of time for everybody who bought a Milli Vanilli album to lose the receipt or to turn into a painfully self-conscious adolescent so enslaved to peer tastes that death would be preferable to admitting having bought "Blame It on the Rain." In a Cook County, Illinois, circuit court, Judge Thomas O'Brien signed off on the refunds ($3 for CDs, $2 for cassettes and $2.50 for concert tickets) but not before grumbling his hope that in the future, courts and lawyers "can devote their time to the resolution of controversies of a more significant social and economic nature." The lawyers—who did all their vocals themselves and played the system like a violin—received $675,000 in fees.

The Queen of Nice Takes a Hike.
When did *Rosie* magazine go wrong and start heading into the land of litigation? Well, there was the July 2001 issue with the cover photo of a decidedly unglamorous O'Donnell in a hospital robe, grimly displaying the bandages on her infected paw for

a story called "Staph Is No Laugh"(hadn't you heard?) at a time when *Rosie*'s sales were already weaker than Gruner + Jahr USA had hoped when it launched the talk-show-host-magazine-that-wasn't-Oprah's in 2001. Then there was that day in May 2002 when O'Donnell quit her talk show, throwing a bit of a wrench into the whole synergistic TV-magazine concept. But all signs pointed to the courtroom a month later, when Gruner + Jahr fired the magazine's editorial chief, hoping to install some-one not quite so cozy with Rosie. An outraged O'Donnell was in-formed that the authority to choose the magazine's editor lay with the publishing company, not with the show-biz professional. So O'Donnell yanked her name off the magazine formerly known as *McCall's*, effectively shutting it down.

With the century-old publication disbanding less than two years after rebranding, all that was left to do was lawyer up and squabble. Gruner + Jahr sued O'Donnell in October 2002 for $100 million, referring to her as a "self-proclaimed 'uber-bitch'" and arguing that her "bizarre and oft-times mean-spirited be-havior soon had the effect of making it difficult, and ultimately impossible, for G+J to continue publishing the magazine." O'Donnell shot back with a $125 million countersuit. "Of course I'm angry," O'Donnell told one interviewer about her tem-peramental nature. "Rage is the foundation of comedy." But a judicious weighing of the facts is the foundation of the legal system. The November 2003 trial closed with the judge stating that neither party was entitled to a dime.

Sir, Your *Bribe* Is Holding on Line One.

In the wake of the destruction from the 1906 San Francisco earthquake, Louis Glass initially looked like a hero. As the general manager of Pacific States Telephone and Telegraph, Glass hustled successfully to get telephone service working again. A year later, Glass was exposed in a bribery scandal that included the city's mayor and most of its board of supervisors. Glass himself was convicted of paying off supervisors to preserve his company's monopoly on phone service in San Francisco, but managed to get the conviction overturned on appeal.

Glass's attempt to profit from the disaster was stupid, but his eventual exoneration should have exempted him from the ranks of dumb-business pioneers, right? True enough, except for the fact that in 1889, Glass built a contraption that would play a tune from a wax-cylinder phonograph if you inserted a nickel in a slot. He's generally recognized as both the inventor of the jukebox and the guy who failed to get rich from the device. For that he deserves some dumb-business recognition, although truth be told, there weren't many pop acts around to record jukebox-ready singles at that point because no one yet had invented the limousine.

Last in the Yellow Pages, First on the D.A.'s To-Do List

In 1986, Barry Minkow seemed to exemplify the American Dream. All of 19 years old, he had created ZZZZ Best, a carpet-cleaning company, and was taking it public. Starting with a $1,600 loan and working out of a Los Angeles garage, Minkow began building his business—his mom worked the phones—and journalists looking for an inspiring, up-by-his-bootstraps story came calling. Oprah featured him, as did *Newsweek*. Tom Bradley, then mayor of L.A., declared a Barry Minkow Day.

When it comes to fraud, it always helps to have a good cover story.

When ZZZZ Best went public in '86—its stock leaping from $4 to $18 a share, with a $200 million market cap—nobody detected, at first, that Minkow was cooking the books. Forty percent profit margins were completely invented, and Minkow became an expert at fake money orders and wall-to-wall credit card fraud. When accountants asked to see a finished carpet-cleaning job, Minkow rented out buildings and rolls of carpet and had ZZZZ Best staffers stationed to look as if they were working on a commissioned job.

A year after the IPO, the jig was up. Minkow was busted and sentenced to 25 years in jail (he served seven and a half) and ordered to pay $26 million to investors.

Once released from prison, Minkow started vacuuming up souls for the Lord as the pastor at a San Diego church. He also began working the lecture circuit, telling corporations how to detect fraud. Proceeds from his four books go to pay off creditors. In the write-about-what-you-know tradition, the books all concern corporate scamming.

Martha Stewart, Multimillionaire Queen of All Media and Housewares, Indicted on June 4, 2003, for Securities Fraud and Obstruction of Justice All Over the Sale of Some ImClone Stock for $229,000

—You can keep all your lines about the thread counts of jail-cell bedsheets, growing cilantro in the exercise yard and the difficulty of looking svelte in an orange jumpsuit. For us at *Business 2.0,* nothing tops giggling over how little it took to send her spit-shined reputation to the compost heap.

My Friend Tino Will Have the Tossed Greens—200 Million of 'Em.

Tino De Angelis knew salad dressing. He also knew basic chemistry. With the simple fact that oil and water don't mix, he was able float a colossal fraud.

In the early 1960s, De Angelis was the president of Allied Crude Vegetable Oil and a major speculator in vegetable oil futures. The one-time butcher from the Bronx—which earned him the nickname "Tough Tino"—boasted that he was one of the country's largest manufacturers of vegetable oil. That earned him the nickname "The Salad Oil King."

Business lesson number one: Don't hand your money to anybody who has more than one nickname.

De Angelis financed his speculating by persuading investors to part with $200 million. He used his salad oil as col-

Legal

lateral, so investors understandably wanted to take a peek at the goods. De Angelis escorted the moneybags to a New Jersey warehouse where they could feast their eyes on an ocean of oil shimmering in vats. For a while, the investors seemed like the dumbbells in this story—they didn't detect that the tanks were actually filled with water and garnished with a splash of vegetable oil that formed a film on top. But ultimately, as is so often the case with massive rip-offs, the perpetrator was revealed as the fathead for thinking he could get away with it. De Angelis got caught and spent seven years dining on prison cafeteria food.

After getting out of jail, De Angelis said it's life on the outside that's tough: "Try to make a living and all the big guys try to shoot you down." Inside? It was "tranquil," he said. Tranquil, like oil poured on troubled—ah, forget it.

Hell Hath No Fury Like a Mummified Vixen Scorned.

Signing Joan Collins to a $4 million deal to write two works of fiction must have seemed like a pretty easy call at Random House in 1990. The TV actress—who had become a pop-culture touchstone of the 1980s as Alexis Carrington on *Dynasty*—had already written four books, including a first novel, *Prime Time*, in 1988. And her sister, Jackie Collins, was so reliably popular with airport-bookstore customers that Joan's sex-'n'-shopping tomes would just be a sort of brand extension.

But then a curious thing happened. Having hired a celebrity writer, Random House suddenly seemed to expect an actual piece of literature. Rejecting the manuscripts Collins eventually submitted, the publisher not only wasn't going to pay her another dime, Random House also wanted its $1.2 million advance back. Testifying in the lawsuit and countersuit that soon followed, Random House editor Joni Evans called the prose for *The Ruling Passion* and *Hell Hath No Fury* "jumbled and disjointed," "dull" and "clichéd." Strong words about manuscripts that included such spirited passages as "'Don't call me your little cabbage,' she said savagely. 'I'm nobody's cabbage.'"

Unfortunately for Random House, it turned out that the publisher had been so captivated by the thought of landing Collins that it had made a terrible misjudgment, agreeing to remove the standard book-contract language stipulating that manuscripts had to be submitted in publishable form. And for this amorous, foolhardy gesture, a Manhattan court determined, Random House had to kiss its advance goodbye—plus another million.

Later that year Collins published a novel about a stylish actress who stars in a prime-time soap opera about a wealthy family. Brought out by Dutton under the title *Infamous*—though *Nobody's Cabbage* does have a nice ring to it—the book was a best-seller.

As Long as You Also Feel Good About a 10x10 Cell and a Roommate Who Insists That You Call Him "Daddy"

"Greed is all right, by the way—I want you to know that. I think greed is healthy. You can be greedy and still feel good about yourself."

—Ivan Boesky, speaking before a group of impressionable business school students at the University of California at Berkeley in 1985. The following year, Boesky was busted in the insider trading scandal that also took down Michael Milken. Boesky served 18 months in prison and paid $100 million in fines.

Let's See, on Our Special Magic Treasure Map to the World's Biggest Gold Deposit, It Says Bre-X Marks the Spot

Canadians loathe the way Americans are always grasping after the next new thing. So it's entirely fitting that while the United States will recall the late 1990s as the era of a delusional investment mania for the Internet, Canada can look on it as a period of delusional investment mania for a good, old-fashioned gold mine.

The tiny Canadian exploration group Bre-X Minerals announced in 1995 that it had some very promising results coming in from Indonesia. Estimates of the gold near the Busang river in Borneo rose steadily over the next couple of years: 1.5 million ounces, 3 million, 10 million, 40 million, 70 million, 200 freakin' million. It would be the biggest gold discovery in history, worth tens of billions of dollars! And cautious investors did what they have always done whenever someone whispers the magic word *gold:* they threw money like a drunk at a strip club. JP Morgan, Merrill Lynch, Fidelity, Republic National Bank and thousands of smaller investors—let's be fair, not just Canadians—piled into Bre-X. The company's stock went from being worth pennies to being worth more than 200 Canadian dollars before a 10-for-one-split in May '96.

And then the gold numbers started sounding a little tinny. The problem with remote jungle mining operations is that they're remote jungle mining operations. It's difficult to monitor test drills and easy to fake results by "salting" samples with, oh, gold scraped from jewelry. Though no one ever proved any connection, at about the time someone other than a Bre-X employee was finally allowed to test the site in 1997, one of Bre-X's main geologists in Borneo died in what was ruled a suicide, falling from a helicopter high above the jungle. The new testing determined there were "insignificant amounts of gold" at Busang. And just like that, Bre-X and the Borneo gold frenzy evaporated. The company that at one time had a market value of $4.5 billion was delisted from the Toronto stock exchange. Bre-Xecutives claimed that they had been duped by workers in the field. But investors went on a fault-finding crusade that is still winding its way through the courts as they try to figure how the most significant gold involved in Bre-X's thrilling discovery was probably in the teeth through which somebody was lying.

What Did He Expect from These Apseholes?

In August 2002, Jim Koch, CEO of Boston Beer Co., paid one of his regular courtesy visits to the New York–based *Opie and Anthony* radio show. Boston Beer, which makes the Samuel Adams brand, was a major sponsor of the syndicated program, and Koch benightedly had signed off on a contest called "Sex for Sam," then in its third year. The concept: have sex in a public place, win all the acclaim that comes with being noticed by infantile shock-jocks. To celebrate Koch's presence, Anthony Cumia and Gregg "Opie" Hughes had a big announcement: they'd persuaded a couple to have sex inside St. Patrick's Cathedral in New York City.

Legal

The Catholic Church, already coping with church-sex problems of its own, was livid about the stunt. The offending couple, visiting from Virginia, and the radio show's producer on the scene were arrested for public lewdness. A week later, Koch took out ads in Boston papers apologizing, and Infinity Broadcasting canceled the *Opie and Anthony* show, ending America's love affair with its other regular features, including the Naughtiest Nightie Contest, the Boob-O-Lantern Contest and the Whipped Cream Bikini Contest. But the legal fallout continued into the fall of 2003. On the day that the couple, Brian Florence and Loretta Harper, was expected to plead guilty to disorderly conduct charges, Florence's lawyer disclosed that his 38-year-old client had died the previous week of heart failure. Both Harper and the the *Opie and Anthony* producer who accompanied the duo eventually pleaded guilty to disorderly conduct and were ordered to perform community service. As for the 13 Infinity-owned radio stations that aired the stunt, they were each fined $27,500 by the FCC.

Would Vous Be Interessai en Quelque Swampland Nous Have Pour Sale in Provence? Or Maybe Notre Deal Magnifique for Le Pont Neuf?

Pulling penny-ante scams on the passengers aboard ocean liners can be nerve-wracking work. Tourists are easy prey, but there's always the lurking problem of finding an escape route in the mid-Atlantic if one of them wises up. So in 1925, grifter Victor Lustig disembarked from a ship in France intent on exploring what he could accomplish, conwise, on solid ground.

He found the Eiffel Tower.

After reading a newspaper article about the monument's crumbling condition, Lustig put together a plan. Posing as the deputy director-general of the Ministry of Posts and Telegraphs, Lustig summoned six scrap-metal dealers for a confidential meeting and slipped them the news: the Eiffel Tower was going to be demolished and sold for scrap. Submit your bids now.

Andre Poisson was the lucky bidder and promptly handed over the equivalent of $125,000 for the Eiffel contract. The deputy director-general of the Ministry of Posts and Telegraphs congratulated the scrap man, wished him luck and fled to Vienna with the money, assuming the gendarmes would be coming around to have a word with him shortly after Monsieur Poisson pulled up on the Champ de Mars to start work.

But the authorities never came. Poisson was too embarrassed to report the scam. Lustig, intrigued, returned to Paris a month later and worked the Eiffel Tower scrap-metal trick again. This time he walked away with $200,000. Wisely quitting while he was ahead, Lustig ditched the Eiffel gambit and returned to America, where he posed as an Austrian count and worked non-scrap-metal-related cons.

"I really don't understand honest people," Lustig once said. "They lead desperate lives, full of boredom." Of course, there's another category of humans who fit that description. Lustig joined their ranks in 1935, when he was convicted of counterfeiting. From then until his death in 1947, the man who sold the Eiffel Tower twice spent his time getting to know another well-known landmark—Alcatraz.

He Might Have Stolen Gretzky from Canada, but That Was Nothing Compared to What He Got from the Bank of America.

For a while there, it looked like Bruce McNall would go down in history as the guy who pried Canadian hockey hero Wayne Gretzky out of Edmonton and managed to make ice hockey hot in Los Angeles. But prison terms have a way of elbowing their way into the first lines of bios. McNall, whose first fortune came from dealing in rare coins, owned racehorses and produced movies (*The Fabulous Baker Boys* in '89 being one of his). He generally reveled in the life of an XXL millionaire, buying three private jets, two helicopters and a handful of houses. But his ownership of the Los Angeles Kings is what made McNall famous. His tireless defrauding of banks is what made him infamous.

Slammed with debts in the early '90s, McNall performed various acts of financial triage both legitimate (selling off part of his Kings stake) and not so legitimate (setting up false accounts, inflating his personal worth and cheating at least six banks out of $236 million). The latter were ill-advised moves, but McNall didn't have a monopoly on idiocy in his dealings. The financial sharpies at Bank of America loaned McNall millions, relying for collateral on the amazing collection of sports memorabilia on display in McNall's office—the star-struck bankers were blown away by the game-worn jerseys of Lou Gehrig and Johnny Bench, and they were awed by Babe Ruth's signed contract. They were so busy swooning, in fact, that the bankers didn't inquire about the actual ownership of the items. Most of them were there on consignment.

After pleading guilty to four fraud-related charges in 1994, McNall served four years in prison-worn jersey number 04302-112.

God Is My Co-pilot? How About My Attorney's Co-counsel? Three Dumb Moments over the Course of 14 Months in the Televangelism Business.

1. In January 1987, Oral Roberts announces to his television audience that he has it on good authority—God, actually—that he will be called "home" if he doesn't raise $8 million by the end of March to finance scholarships for his medical school. After numerous critics, both faithful and not, question Roberts's claim, he angrily commands his followers "to put on the holy armor of God." It looks as if the preacher had better start packing his bags for the trip home when donations lag, but then a dog-track owner in Sarasota, Florida, makes up the difference just in time. Later that year, Roberts speaks before a congressional subcommittee investigating questionable fund-raising practices of media ministries. A backpedaling Roberts explains that the Lord never cited an exact dollar target.

2. In March 1987, Jim Bakker, head of the $129-million-a-year PTL (Praise the Lord, *not* Pass the Loot) ministry, confesses that he had sex with a church secretary, Jessica Hahn, and resigns. As the PTL empire—including the Heritage USA Christian theme park in South Carolina—careens into bankruptcy, a criminal investigation reveals that Bakker paid Hahn $265,000 in hush money and diverted $3.7 million in PTL donations for

his own personal use (which included commissioning the construction of an air-conditioned doghouse for the family pet). TV viewers lament the demise of the PTL talk show, taking with it Bakker's wife and mascara-mad co-host, Tammy Faye Bakker. In October 1989, Bakker is found guilty on nine counts of fraud and conspiracy; U.S. District Judge Robert "Maximum Bob" Potter sentences him to 45 years in prison and orders him to pay $500,000 in fines. Paroled five years later, a divorced Bakker is subsequently spotted preaching in Los Angeles ghetto missions.

3. In February 1988, Jimmy Swaggart—who'd worked overtime in 1987 denouncing Bakker's PTL transgressions—publicly admits consorting with a New Orleans prostitute. After his ouster from the Assemblies of God, Swaggart sees the audience for his $150-million-a-year TV ministry drop 50 percent by year's end. In 1991, a court rules that, because he spread falsehoods about the sex habits of rival preacher Marvin Gorman, Swaggart must pay Gorman $6.4 million in damages. The debt apparently doesn't put much of a crimp in Swaggart's cash expenditures. Later that year, the televangelist is again caught by Earth-bound authorities paying a professional sinner to fornicate with him.

CHAPTER NINE

INFORMATION TECHNOLOGY

> The tech boom has, as promised, made business much, much more efficient. Now companies can screw up faster, on a more massive scale, than ever before. Plus, there are all those e-mail breadcrumbs that lead investigators right to your door.

Good News: Speaking Gibberish No Impediment to Making Billions

"We don't have the user-centricity. Until we understand context, which is way beyond presence—presence is the most trivial notion of context."

—Microsoft chairman Bill Gates, in 2002, explaining his company's .Net initiative. Or trying to explain, anyway.

When It Absolutely, Positively Has to Be There Soonish

It's easy to become inured to blather about how the Internet has changed the world. So it's useful sometimes to reflect on exactly how life has been altered in the past 20 years. Consider the difference between sending an urgent message today versus the mid-1980s.

Today:

1. Open e-mail program.
2. Write message.
3. Click SEND.

In 1984:

1. Write message.
2. Call Federal Express.
3. Wait for Federal Express courier to arrive.
4. Give message to Federal Express courier.
5. Wait as Federal Express courier drives your urgent message to the nearest Federal Express office.
6. Wait as Federal Express courier, at Federal Express office, faxes message to the Federal Express office closest to your chosen destination.
7. Wait as Federal Express courier at destination takes message from the Federal Express office to the person you wish to receive your urgent message.
8. Pay $35.

Launched in the summer of 1984, ZapMail was the darling of Federal Express planners. The company spent $100 million on start-up costs and planned to lay out $1.2 billion over 10 years to set up a satellite transmission service. That was a reasonable expense, according to the FedExperts, because the company anticipated annual revenues of $1.33 billion from ZapMail by 1988. When everybody realized—by, say, 1995—that ZapMail was the only way to send messages quickly, annual revenues would reach a whopping $3.53 billion.

The operating costs, unfortunately, were massive, and Federal Express saw a 71 percent drop in profits in the quarter it launched ZapMail—but hey, that's the price you pay for single-handedly shifting a paradigm. James L. Barksdale promised that ZapMail would break even "within a few years." We'll never know—the company abandoned the program in November 1986.

Wall Street sent an urgent message of thanks: Federal Express stock rose $8.25 the day the company announced ZapMail's demise.

Of Course Not. We'll All Have ZapMail.

"There is no reason for any individual to have a computer in their home."

—Ken Olson, then president of Digital Equipment Corporation, at the 1977 convention of the World Future Society

This Personal Computer Thing? It's Just a Fad. Doesn't Anybody Listen to Ken Olson?

In 1980, IBM was in a hurry, which may be why they didn't have the time to look at the large THINK signs that famously festooned the corporate headquarters. All IBM knew was that it wanted to get in on the market for those newfangled "personal" computers. Which created a fine opportunity for a geeky Harvard dropout living in Redmond, Washington, to kneecap Big Blue.

Realizing that it didn't have the ability to develop a processor or an operating system, IBM outsourced the jobs. For the processor, it went to a small outfit called Intel. For the OS, it went to Microsoft, a company that happily partnered with IBM even though it did not, in fact, have an OS to sell.

Microsoft owner Bill Gates scrambled and found the QDOS (Quick and Dirty Operating System) at Seattle Computer Products, where founder Tim Paterson offered the program for a flat fee of $50,000. Microsoft rushed back to IBM with the freshly renamed MS-DOS, which Gates made available with one condition: let Microsoft sell the system to other vendors.

To which IBM in effect said, "Are you kidding? And let your pathetic start-up smear our august company across the blacktop of business history? No chance, pal." Just a little joke. No, IBM figured there wasn't much to lose on this one, estimating it would take five years to sell even 250,000 PCs. IBM, in fact, sold three 3 million units in that time span. Despite the massive success, IBM soon noticed that with Microsoft—as well as Intel—free to market their wares to Dell, Compaq and others, its market share was eroding. By 2001, IBM sales had fallen to third place in the PC race. Thanks in no small part to one of the most eye-popping, chuckleheaded giveaways in tech history, Microsoft's market capitalization today is $285.5 billion—more than double IBM's $141.7.

MSNBC: The Network You Trust to Spell "Shiite" Correctly

"It's not the first time it's happened, but hopefully it's the last."

—Republican party consultant Niger Innis during an MSNBC interview in February 2002, in response to interviewer Gregg Jarrett's profuse apologies after he discovered an on-screen misspelling of Innis's first name. Yes, *that* misspelling. No word on whether technicians were able to install a slur check feature to avoid future embarrassment.

From a Sharp Mind Comes . . . Well, Divx.

Some people like to rent movies. Others like to buy them. In the late 1990s, Circuit City decided to split the difference and invented a confusing, privacy-invading system with an unpronounceable name that offered the worst of both worlds.

Divx—short for Digital Video Express—was the brainchild of Richard L. Sharp, CEO of electronics retailer Circuit City. Launched in 1998, Divx players worked similarly to DVD machines, but with a few pretzel-like twists:

Renting a Divx video cost $4.99, after which you had only 48 hours to watch the movie.

Want to watch it again? Three more dollars.

Want to say, "Screw this idiotic pricing structure," and just buy the damn disc? Fifteen more dollars.

And, for that extra Big Brother feeling, once a month the Divx machine connected via modem to inform the company of what videos you were renting, rewatching or buying, so it could charge your credit card.

How much would you pay for this snooping piece of video technology? Divx players cost about $100 more than the increasingly popular DVD players. But the benefit, Sharp explained, was that it allowed you to "create your own home video rental store."

But it appears that most people don't want to turn their own homes into video stores, even if it meant not having to put up with sullen twentysomething Fellini experts at the counter and creepy old men ogling the porn boxes in back. Circuit City deep-sixed Divx in 1999, writing off $114 million.

Don't Freak Us Out, Man.

"I don't understand how somebody can be here, then not be here. It's incomprehensible."

—Oracle CEO Larry Ellison, in 2000, plumbing the mysteries of human mortality. An even freakier here/not-here conundrum: how technology can be unbelievably expensive one minute and totally obsolete the next. It's incomprehensible.

But They Got to Open a Totally High-Tech Weight Room with All the Excess Inventory.

You might think that the word *hypergrowth* was coined, oh, sometime in the 1990s, but it originated a decade earlier as a description of Adam Osborne's Silicon Valley misadventures. If anybody had bothered to learn his lesson, a certain bubble might not have gotten *quite* so puffy.

In June 1981, Osborne announced the creation of his PC, the Osborne 1. Not only was it cheaper than the first-to-market Apples, it was also portable. Or, rather, "portable." The thing weighed 23 pounds and was a homely looking contraption with a wee five-inch screen. One critic said it looked like a "drunken sewing machine." But the public apparently found persuasive an Osborne ad campaign that featured two businessmen: one on the left lugging a regulation briefcase, the other (who must have been pretty buff) an Osborne. "The guy on the left," read the copy, "doesn't stand a chance." Sales jumped from $5.8 million in '81 to $68.8 million in '83, when Osborne was moving 10,000 units a month. The founder boasted of a 25-month backlog of orders.

That backlog of Osborne 1 orders—and all attendant revenue—evaporated when the company announced the imminent release of the Osborne Executive, the second-generation portable computer, touted as a huge step up from the Osborne 1. Salivating customers didn't need convincing; they promptly canceled their Osborne 1 orders and awaited the Executive. And waited. With no money coming in and problems plaguing the Executive, that imminent release was pushed back repeatedly. Meanwhile, new Osborne 1's were piling up in inventory. Finally, in September 1983, the company founder made another sort of executive decision: Osborne Computer, $23 million in the red, filed for bankruptcy. News photographers rushed to the company's Hayward, California, headquarters to snap pictures of Osborne, who was using a handy old-school briefcase to cover his face.

Gosh, Craig, That's *So* Exciting. Tell Us More.

"Soon, there will be no such thing as Internet companies. All companies will be Internet companies."

—Intel CEO Craig Barrett, making a speech in London in June 1999

Careful with That SEND Button, Buddy.

One day in late 2000, when it had become increasingly clear that the dotcom bubble was bursting, Merrill Lynch analyst Henry Blodget—famous for predicting that Amazon.com would hit 400—was busy reading his e-mail. Forwarded an article on Infospace that bemoaned the "horror story" of its annual report, Blodget—who had rated Infospace's stock a "buy"—shot a message to his research team. "Can we please reset this stupid price target and rip this piece of junk off whatever list it's on," he wrote. "If you have to downgrade it, downgrade it." Later, an analyst forwarded a negative article about 24/7, another Internet company on the skids; Blodget dismissed the stock, rated a "buy" by Merrill, as a "piece of shit."

As revealed by Blodget's intraoffice e-mails—which were subpoenaed by a New York State attorney general investigation—designation as a "piece of shit" or, rather more snappily, "POS," didn't affect the company's stance on a stock. In a December 2000 e-mail, Blodget denigrated the dotcom Life-Minders by saying, "I can't believe what a POS that thing is." Merrill Lynch customers, on the other hand, probably wouldn't have been able to believe that the firm later sold the stock as "an attractive investment." Under increasing pressure from authorities, Merrill Lynch agreed to pay a $100 million fine in May 2002. Blodget resigned from the firm in 2001; in April 2003, he agreed to pay $4 million in fines and was permanently barred by the National Association of Securities Dealers (NASD).

After Millions of Dollars and Years of Research, Dean Kamen Brings You . . . the Hype Machine!

"More significant than the World Wide Web."

—Venture capitalist John Doerr, who invested heavily in the development of Kamen's Segway Human Transporter

"If enough people see the machine, you won't have to convince them to architect cities around it. It'll just happen."

—Apple CEO and early Segway enthusiast Steve Jobs

"[The Segway] will sweep over the world and change lives, cities and ways of thinking."

—Author Steve Kemper, explaining the Segway—also called "Ginger," also called "IT"—in a book proposal that was allegedly leaked in January 2001 and touched off a techno-orgy of speculation

"You'll have no problem selling it. The question is, are people going to be allowed to use it?"

—Amazon.com chief Jeff Bezos. By mid-2003, the answer was in: Not really. Many cities tightly regulated Segways in what amounted to an outright ban.

"Several thousand."

—Segway COO Doug Field, in June 2003, on just how many had actually been sold via Amazon.com, the primary Segway source, since being made available to the presumably clamoring public the previous fall

The Weird Thing Is No One Would Touch the Stock Certificates AOL Wanted to Hand Out.

In the summer of 2001, firefights in the long-running cola wars had flared up anew. Pepsi had Britney Spears in its corner; Coca-Cola had Christina Aguilera. Coke then forged an alliance with America Online and opened a new front in the battle: a contest in which AOL users would be asked to answer a question about an Aguilera song (probably meaning they'd have to want the money badly enough to borrow a preteen's MP3 player to listen to the song) and then click on a virtual Coke bottle cap to see if they'd won $10,000.

Thanks to a case of computer-assisted corporate cross-promotion gone awry, several hundred desperate people were mistakenly told they had bagged the dough. Coke, not interested in the option of buying the loyalty of the nonwinning winners for a few million dollars, insisted that AOL clean up the mess. AOL offered the victims a $200 gift certificate from Target or Amazon, plus three free months of AOL and entry in another contest with the same prize money. Though, God willing, not the same soundtrack. Advantage: Pepsi.

Agreed.

"We screwed up."

—Rob Glaser, CEO of online media delivery firm RealNetworks, after admitting in 1999 that it was secretly tracking the listening habits of users of its RealJukebox software

Memo to Glaser: Next Time, Hire Denis Zerkin to Prepare Your Statement.

In November 2002, subscribers to the "Virus News" e-mail dispatch from Russian antivirus software company Kaspersky Labs received an important alert about a damaging new computer worm making the rounds. Users were told to keep an eye out for the "Braid worm," which could debilitate PCs.

How to recognize the nefarious virus? A close examination of the Kaspersky e-mail itself would have been a good place to start. It was unwittingly sent out with the worm embedded.

Kaspersky Labs announced that it was the victim of hackers who had obtained the "Virus News" mailing list—not exactly the sort of admission that customers like to hear from an Internet security firm. But the company rejected suggestions that the Braid-distribution gaffe had dented its reputation. In fact, according to Director of Marketing Denis Zerkin, the whole episode was downright flattering: "This case shows that Kaspersky Labs is growing and becoming more and more famous and attracts more attentions from the hackers."

Let's Go to Vegas—Nobody Looks for Dodgy Scam Artists There.

While some companies might throw themselves a party featuring a really good cover band with a repertoire that included songs by the Who, Kiss, the Dixie Chicks and Tony Bennett, Pixelon founder Michael Adam Fenne decided that just wouldn't be good enough for his dotcom launch party in October 1999. So he *hired* the Who, Kiss, the Dixie Chicks and Tony Bennett to perform at his $12 million weekend-long orgy of self-congratulation at the MGM Grand Hotel in Las Vegas. Fenne was blowing nearly a third of his venture capital in the name of fun, but 1999 was a different time—some of the entertainers agreed to be paid in Pixelon stock—and Fenne tirelessly spread the word that Pixelon had developed some slam-dunk Web videoconferencing software. A lot of people couldn't hear him, though; Pixelon's notoriously buggy product torpedoed the launch-celebration Webcast.

Still, it was a hell of a party.

"I just wanted to own the city for this weekend," Fenne told reporters.

Pixelon's board of directors just wanted to disown him afterward. They ousted Fenne the following month, and an amusing story about late-'90s NASDAQ hubris might have ended there. But did we mention that 1999 was a different time? If Pixelon's board members or investors had performed a background check on Fenne, they might have turned up the info that "Fenne" was the *nom de dotcom* of David Kim Stanley, a convicted felon who'd been on Virginia's most-wanted list for allegedly swindling $1.25 million dollars out of Virginia and Tennessee residents in an investment scam. On the run from investigators, Stanley dyed his hair blond, transformed himself into Fenne and headed to San Juan Capistrano, California, to start Pixelon. In April 2000, Stanley turned himself in to authorities. He claimed he was still working for Pixelon as a consultant, which the company denied, but at that late stage it was a moot point: a month later, Pixelon collapsed.

But the company's demise didn't mean the end of Stanley. Two years after the infamous Vegas extravaganza, he was running StatGuard, a Web-cam security company he'd co-founded from a jail cell in Sullivan County, Tennessee. It was a tribute to human tenacity in the face of demonstrated criminal folly. And proof that, although the characters and companies change across the decades, dumb moments in business have lost none of their power to make us weep with gratitude that—dim though we might be—thank God we didn't do *that*.

ACKNOWLEDGMENTS

The Dumbest Moments franchise, if you can call it that, never would have grown into book form—or in other words, *metastasized*—if Tim Carvell hadn't been around long ago to co-create the idea as a feature article for *Business 2.0* with Adam Horowitz and then co-author the first two annual lists. Likewise, Ned Desmond and Jim Aley (former editor and managing editor, respectively) not only didn't shoot down the proposed feature but also contributed their own pitiless criticisms and witticisms to its early incarnations.

Compiling a year's worth of Dumbest Moments is child's play compared to trying to pin down an all-time list. Many thanks to Sarah Stebbins and Vanessa Gould for their tireless sifting through the soul-sapping annals of business history to turn up the choicest nuggets of fool's gold.

We called dozens and dozens of business professors, authors and other experts to talk about their favorite dumb moments in business history, and some of them actually agreed to speak to us. (It was a mixed blessing. You long to be put on hold when a certain academic who shall remain nameless launches into his stand-up routine about a particular passage of the Sherman Anti-Trust Act that could have been written with greater clarity.) Some of the folks listed below were more helpful—and *much* funnier—than others, but we want to send a big wet mwah! to each and every one:

- Ben Branch, professor of finance at the University of Massachusetts at Amherst, and bankruptcy trustee for Bank of New England and manager of VFB LLC

Acknowledgments

- Arnold C. Cooper, Louis A. Weil Jr. professor of management at the Krannert School of Management at Purdue University
- Robert A. Eisenbeis, senior vice president and director of research at the Federal Reserve Bank of Atlanta
- Sydney Finkelstein, Steven Roth professor of management at Dartmouth College's Tuck School of Business
- Dale L. Flesher, associate dean and professor at the University of Mississippi's Patterson School of Accountancy
- Tony Freyer, university research professor of history and law at the University of Alabama School of Law
- Kathryn Harrigan, Henry R. Kravis professor of business leadership at the Columbia Business School
- Stefanie Lenway, associate dean for MBA programs at the Carlson School of Management at the University of Minnesota, Minneapolis
- Lynn M. LoPucki, Security Pacific Bank professor of law at the UCLA School of Law
- Gerald Meyers, adjunct professor at the School of Business Administration at the University of Michigan, Ann Arbor
- Jon Moen, associate professor of economics at the University of Mississippi
- Christine Rosen, associate professor at the Haas School of Business at the University of California, Berkeley
- Jim Seward, associate professor of finance and Prochnow fellow in finance at the University of Wisconsin–Madison School of Business
- Jim Smith, professor of finance at the University of North Carolina's Kenan-Flagler School of Business

INDEX

Animals
 Noncute, anthropomorphizing-
  resistant variety slain by
  Disney employees, 122–23
 Shredded, 69
Ax
 Wielding no impediment to
  shopping experience, 71–72
  (see also *Hatchet*)

Babies
 Can take a hike if they're going
  to mewl about secondhand
  smoke, 63–64 (see also
  Cigarettes)
 Delivery of facilitated by fetal
  exposure to nicotine, 63
 Hoodwinked by pitiless baby-
  food giant, 36
Beer drinkers
 Draw line at guzzling chemical-
  laced brew that makes stein
  look like snow globe,
  41–42
 Flock to dismal ballgame to
  guzzle 10-cent brews, dis-
  robe, riot, 72–73
 Flock to dismal ballgame,
  watch explosion, riot,
  73–75
Boss and employee, difficult
 Rosie O'Donnell is a (see also
  Putting It Nicely, That's),
  124–25

Box, the
 Thinking outside, looks good
  on paper, not store shelves,
  5–6
 Thinking outside, results in
  bizarre, offensive *and* expensive promotion, 4–5 (see
  also *Kenyans*)
Budget, enormous film production
 Not recouped at box office,
  49, 60–63
Business school, case studies
  taught at
 Involving cars, 97–98
 Involving PC operating systems, 142–43
 Involving soda, 98–99
 Involving tulip bulbs, 95–
  97

Cabbage
 Joan Collins is nobody's little
  (see also *Contract, nonstan-
  dard*), 129–30
Canada
 Got some crooked hosers up
  there too, eh?, 131–32
Carmaker
 Pioneers used-car sales ethics
  in new-car sales, 82–83
Cellular phones
 Manufacturer's brainstorm:
  bigger, more expensive is
  way to go, 91–93

Index

Index

Index

God
    Alleged to have told Oral
        Roberts to raise $8 million
        or else, 136
Government, U.S.
    Fleeced, by corporate America
        (see also just about any
        damned thing being deliv-
        ered to a federal loading
        dock), 5
Gull-wing car doors
    Mysterious obsession of
        second-rate automakers
        with, 38–39, 47–49

Hand, importance of knowing
        what other is doing
    To avoid paying twice for same
        album, 14–15
Hatchet
    Novel use in linguistic hairsplit-
        ting by thin-skinned flack,
        71–72
Herb
    Annoying character seemingly
        created as double agent
        for McDonald's bent on
        destroying Burger King,
        101–2
Hitler
    Even worse than Herb as
        brand enhancer,
        106–7
Hoover
    Where's J. Edgar when you
        need him to investigate
        $30 million idiocy of like-
        named vacuum company?,
        104–5

Illness
    Sensation of not necessarily
        sign that product is bad for
        you, 67
Industry, importance of
        understanding before
        entering
    To avoid creating garbage
        bags that haulers won't
        touch, 49–50
    To avoid creating garbage
        barge that local govern-
        ments won't let touch their
        shores, 105–6
Innovation, brilliant
    Handed off to competition for
        zero cash dollars, 9–10
Innovation, dubious
    Colorized movies, 39–41
        (see also a nice black-
        and-white print of
        Casablanca, with some
        fresh popcorn)
    Hernia-inducing "portable"
        computers, 145–46
    Trudging ZapMail, 140–41
    Wet toilet paper, 7–9 (see also
        Excrement)
Internal Revenue Service
    Makes Willie Nelson personal
        troubadour, 112–13

Jargon, incomprehensible
    Catnip for investors—perpetual
        motion, 11–12
Job preservation, attempt at
        CEO puts smiley face
        on financial meltdown,
        109

Index

Index